DISCIPLE for LIFE

Ephesians

YOUR IDENTITY IN CHRIST

Tony Merida

LifeWay Press®
Nashville, Tennessee

Published by LifeWay Press® • © 2016 Tony Merida

No part of this book may be reproduced or transmitted in any form or by any means, electronic or mechanical, including photocopying and recording, or by any information storage or retrieval system, except as may be expressly permitted in writing by the publisher. Requests for permission should be addressed in writing to LifeWay Press®; One LifeWay Plaza; Nashville, TN 37234-0152.

ISBN 978-1-4300-6552-4 • Item 005792212

Dewey decimal classification: 227.5
Subject headings: BIBLE. N.T. EPHESIANS \ CHRISTIAN LIFE \ DISCIPLESHIP

Unless indicated otherwise, Scripture quotations are taken from The Holy Bible, English Standard Version® (ESV®), copyright © 2001 by Crossway, a publishing ministry of Good News Publishers. Used by permission. All rights reserved. . Scripture quotations marked NIV are taken from the Holy Bible, NEW INTERNATIONAL VERSION®. Copyright © 1973, 1978, 1984 by Biblica Inc. All rights reserved worldwide. Used by permission.

To order additional copies of this resource, write to LifeWay Resources Customer Service; One LifeWay Plaza; Nashville, TN 37234-0113; fax 615.251.5933; call toll free 800.458.2772; order online at *lifeway.com;* email *orderentry@lifeway.com;* or visit the LifeWay Christian Store serving you.

Printed in the United States of America

Groups Ministry Publishing • LifeWay Resources • One LifeWay Plaza • Nashville, TN 37234-0152

Contents

About the Authors

Tony Merida is the founding pastor of Imago Dei Church in Raleigh, North Carolina. He also serves as an associate professor of preaching at Southeastern Baptist Theological Seminary in Wake Forest, North Carolina. He's the author of several books, including *Ordinary: How to Turn the World Upside Down.*

Ben Reed adapted Tony Merida's study of the Book of Ephesians for small groups. Ben is the lead small-groups pastor at the Lake Forest campus of Saddleback Church in Orange County, California. Having led small-group ministries at a variety of different churches, he thrives on building healthy, biblical, authentic, life-changing communities.

Introduction

Most of us think we searched for and found our identity during our teenage or college years. But in reality many of us are still trying to find it. When we don't get the promotion at work, we spiral into an emotional wasteland. When our pants fit a little more snugly than they used to, we freak out. When someone questions whether the talent we're reputed to be good at is truly good, we're shaken to our core.

The Book of Ephesians has an abundance of wisdom to share with us that will reveal where our identity should be anchored. When we anchor our identity in Christ, the shifting winds of change that inevitably happen in life won't sink our ship.

Over the next six weeks we'll look at these topics from Ephesians:

1. "The Struggle in Ephesus": where our identity is centered
2. "New Life in Christ": our identity reconciled with God
3. "New Life in Community": our identity reconciled with people
4. "Pursuing Unity in Christ": our identity unified in the local church
5. "Pursuing Holiness in Christ": how our identity shapes our behavior
6. "Be Strong in Christ": the war against our identity

My prayer is that everyone will dig deeply into the truths of Scripture as we pursue honesty with ourselves and our small groups. The more we're vulnerable with our weaknesses, the closer and safer our groups will become. The closer and safer our groups become, the healthier we'll become, and the more we'll begin living in the freedom and strength of our identity in Christ.

How to Use This Study

This Bible study book includes six weeks of content. Each week has an introductory page summarizing the focus of the week's study, followed by content designed for groups and individuals.

GROUP SESSIONS

Regardless of the day of the week your group meets, each week of content begins with the group session. This group session is designed to be one hour or more, with approximately 15 to 20 minutes of teaching and 45 minutes of personal interaction. It's even better if your group is able to meet longer than an hour, allowing more time for participants to interact with one another.

Each group session uses the following format to facilitate simple yet meaningful interaction among group members, with God's Word, and with the video teaching by a group of trusted pastors.

Start

This page includes questions to get the conversation started and to introduce the video segment.

Watch

This page includes key points from the video teaching, along with space for taking notes as participants watch the video.

Discuss

These two pages include questions and statements that guide the group to respond to the video teaching and to relevant Bible passages.

Pray

This final page of each group session includes a prompt for a closing time of prayer together and space for recording prayer requests of group members.

INDIVIDUAL DISCOVERY

Each *Disciple for Life* small-group resource provides individuals with optional activities during the week, appealing to different learning styles, schedules, and levels of engagement. These options include a plan for application and accountability, a Scripture-reading plan with journaling prompts, a devotion, and two personal studies. You can choose to take advantage of some or all of the options provided.

This Week's Plan

Immediately following the group session's prayer page is a weekly plan offering guidance for everyone to engage with that week's focal point, regardless of a person's maturity level or that week's schedule.

Read

A daily reading plan is outlined for Scriptures related to the group session. Space for personal notes is also provided. Instructions for using the HEAR journaling method for reading Scripture can be found on pages 8–11.

Reflect

A one-page devotional option is provided each week to help members reflect on a biblical truth related to the group session.

Personal Study

Two personal studies are provided each week to take individuals deeper into Scripture and to supplement the biblical truths introduced in the teaching time. These pages challenge individuals to grow in their understanding of God's Word and to make practical application to their lives.

LEADER GUIDE

Pages 120–31 at the back of this book contain a guide that develops a leader's understanding of the thought process behind questions and suggests ways to engage members at different levels of life-changing discussion.

The HEAR Journaling Method for Reading Scripture

Daily Bible Reading

Disciple for Life small-group Bible studies include a daily reading plan for each week. Making time in a busy schedule to focus on God through His Word is a vital part of the Christian life. If you're unable to do anything else provided in your Bible study book during a certain week, try to spend a few minutes in God's Word. The verse selections will take you deeper into stories and concepts that support the teaching and discussion during that week's group session.

Why Do You Need a Plan?

When you're a new believer or at various other times in your life, you may find yourself in a place where you don't know where to begin reading your Bible or how to personally approach Scripture. You may have tried the open-and-point method when you simply opened your Bible and pointed to a verse, hoping to get something out of the random selection from God's Word. Reading random Scriptures won't provide solid biblical growth any more then eating random food from your pantry will provide solid physical growth.

An effective plan must be well balanced for healthy growth. When it comes to reading the Bible, *well balanced* and *effective* mean reading and applying. A regular habit is great, but simply checking a box off your task list when you've completed your daily reading isn't enough. Knowing more about God is also great, but simply reading for spiritual knowledge still isn't enough. You also want to respond to what you're reading by taking action as you listen to what God is saying. After all, it's God's Word.

To digest more of the Word, *Disciple for Life* small-group Bible studies not only provide a weekly reading plan but also encourage you to use a simplified version of the HEAR journaling method. (If this method advances your personal growth, check out *Foundations: A 260-Day Bible-Reading Plan for Busy Believers* by Robby and Kandi Gallaty.)

Journaling What You HEAR in God's Word

You may or may not choose to keep a separate journal in addition to the space provided in this book. A separate journal would provide extra space as well as the opportunity to continue your journal after this study is completed. The HEAR journaling method promotes reading the Bible with a life-transforming purpose. You'll read in order to understand and respond to God's Word.

The HEAR acronym stands for *highlight, explain, apply,* and *respond.* Each of these four steps creates an atmosphere for hearing God speak. After settling on a reading plan, like the one provided in this book in the "Read" section each week, establish a time for studying God's Word. Then you'll be ready to HEAR from God.

Before You Begin: The Most Important Step

To really HEAR God speak to you through His Word, always begin your time with prayer. Pause and sincerely ask God to speak to you. It's absolutely imperative that you seek God's guidance in order to understand His Word (see 1 Cor. 2:12-14). Every time you open your Bible, pray a simple prayer like the one David prayed: "Open my eyes so that I may contemplate wonderful things from Your instruction" (Ps. 119:18).

H = Highlight

After praying for the Holy Spirit's guidance, open this book to the week's reading plan, open a journal if you'd like more space than this book provides, and open your Bible. For an illustration let's assume you're reading Philippians 4:10-13. Verse 13 may jump out and speak to you as something you want to remember, so you'd simply highlight that verse in your Bible.

If keeping a HEAR journal, on the top line write the Scripture reference and the date and make up a title to summarize the meaning of the passage. Then write the letter H and record the verse that stood out and that you highlighted in your Bible. This practice will make it easy to look back through your journal to find a passage you want to revisit in the future.

E = Explain

After you've highlighted your verse(s), explain what the text means. Most simply, how would you summarize this passage in your own words? By asking some simple questions, with the help of God's Spirit, you can understand the meaning of the passage or verse. (A good study Bible can help answer more in-depth questions as you learn to explain a passage of Scripture.) Here are a few good questions to get you started:

- Why was the verse or passage written?
- To whom was it originally written?
- How does the verse or passage fit with the verses before and after it?
- Why would the Holy Spirit include this passage in the Bible book?
- What does God intend to communicate through the text?

If keeping a HEAR journal, below the H write the letter E and explain the text in your own words. Record any answers to questions that help you understand the passage of Scripture.

A = Apply

At this point you're beginning the process of discovering the specific personal word God has for you from His Word. What's important is that you're engaging with the text and wrestling with the meaning. Application is the heart of the process. Everything you've done so far coalesces under this heading. As you've done before, answer a series of questions to discover the significance of these verses to you personally, questions like:

- How can this verse or passage help me?
- What's God saying to me?
- What would the application of this verse look like in my life?

These questions bridge the gap between the ancient world and your world today. They provide a way for God to speak to you through the specific passage or verse.

If keeping a HEAR journal, write the letter A under the letter E, where you wrote a short summary explaining the text. Challenge yourself to write between two and five sentences about the way the text applies to your life.

R = Respond

Finally, you'll respond to the text. A personal response may take on many forms. You may write an action step to do, describe a change in perspective, or simply respond in prayer to what you've learned. For example, you may ask for help in being bold or generous, you may need to repent of unconfessed sin, or you may need to praise God. Keep in mind that you're responding to what you've just read.

In this book or in your journal, record your personal application of each passage of Scripture. You may want to write a brief explanation-and-application summary: "The verse means _____ , so I can or will _____."

If keeping a HEAR journal, write the letter R, along with the way you'll respond to what you highlighted, explained, and applied.

Notice that all the words in the HEAR method are action words: *highlight, explain, apply, respond.* God doesn't want us to sit back and wait for Him to drop truth into our laps. God wants us to actively pursue Him instead of waiting passively. Jesus said:

> Keep asking, and it will be given to you. Keep searching, and you
> will find. Keep knocking, and the door will be opened to you.
> **Matthew 7:7**

The Struggle
in Ephesus

Week 1

Ephesians contains only six chapters. It's a mere 155 verses. If you read it straight through, it would take you about 20 minutes. Yet the rich wisdom packed in this book will take you much longer than 20 minutes to apply and live out. If you want to apply this book, read it slowly. And often.

Paul, the author, writing to the people in Ephesus, started out with a few seemingly benign statements. They would be easy for a reader to gloss over in an attempt to get to "the important stuff." But if you do that, you'll regret it. You'll short-circuit the work God wants to do in your heart instead of digging deeply into who God declared you to be. And who God declared you to be is more powerful than who you feel you are.

The One on whom you fix your eyes is both the source and the object of your identity.

It may seem obvious, but in order to follow Jesus as His disciple, you have to see Him as He truly is. Once you have a clear picture of Jesus, you can fully understand who you are.

Start

Welcome everyone to session 1 of *Ephesians*. Use the following content to begin your group session together.

When you were a kid, what did you want to be when you grew up?

What similarities exist between what you do now and what you thought you wanted to do?

As kids, we dreamed. We dreamed of one day playing professional sports, traveling the universe as an astronaut, or being a superhero who can fly.

Deep down we have a desire to do something significant and make a difference in the world. And there's nothing wrong with that desire. There's actually something God-honoring in it. The hero or heroine's story touches us deeply because God wired us for significance. The deeper questions we all have to answer are what define who we are and where we'll find our significance.

In this first session Tony Merida will introduce us to the Book of Ephesians by starting where Paul started the letter: defining our identity.

Pray that God will open your hearts and minds as you watch video session 1.

Watch

Use the space below to follow along and take notes as you watch video session 1.

If your _____ is not in Christ, you will be dissatisfied. You were made for a relationship with God through Christ.

When you become a _____, you become a new person. You get a new identity.

We have to keep feeding our souls with _____.

Are you enjoying the _____ of being in Christ?

You need your _____ to be enthralled with the Person and work of Jesus Christ.

If you love Jesus deeply, it will change your _____ dramatically.

Discuss

Use the following statements and questions to discuss the video.

The most basic yet important question you can ask yourself right now is "Am I in Christ?" The Book of Ephesians is an amazing place to discover who Jesus is and who He created you to be.

> **How have you seen someone's behavior change when they started a new relationship?**

> **How does your relationship with Jesus change the way you live your life?**

> **If you've been following Jesus for a number of years, how have things changed since your early years of faith?**

Read Ephesians 1:1-2 aloud with the group.

Paul, an apostle, wrote this book and started his greeting with the words "Grace to you and peace ..." (v. 2).

> **How does knowing you're covered in grace and peace affect the way you see yourself?**

When we read the Bible, we may feel there's a great detachment between the lives of the people in Scripture and our lives. But the culture Paul described in the Book of Ephesians is hauntingly similar to ours today.

> **In what things (for example, activities, behaviors, relationships, personas) does culture tell us to find our identity?**

According to the video, what did the apostle Paul do in an effort to change the culture in Ephesus? What happened as a result?

How should living in the reality of a new identity change the way you—

interact at work?

receive criticism?

view success?

vacation?

It's easy to see following God as a relationship that limits what we do in life. As you read the Bible, you see the Ten Commandments and a slew of other rules that keep you from doing things. You may be tempted to say, "I wish God would let me …" But the reality is that being a follower of Jesus and rooting our identity in Him afford us many privileges.

As a follower of Christ whose identity is rooted in Him, what privileges do you have that others don't?

As we dive in to this first week's study, you may have some apprehensions. Or excitement. Or questions.

What are your hopes or expectations for this study of Ephesians?

We all have hopes and expectations in starting this study. God has hopes and expectations for us too.

Conclude the group session with the prayer activity on the following page.

Pray

Each week we'll conclude the group session with two actions.

1. We'll consider our responses to the truth of Scripture and pray for the Holy Spirit to work in our lives in ways we've seen in God's Word.

2. We'll pray for one another, particularly in relation to applying the biblical truths studied and discussed during the group session.

   In what ways do you need the grace and peace Paul mentioned in his greeting to the Christians in Ephesus (see Eph. 1:2)?

   How will you think or act differently as a result of what God has revealed in His Word?

Spend a few minutes praying for each person in the group. Ask God to reveal Himself and speak clearly to each person during the next six weeks.

Prayer Requests

Encourage members to complete "This Week's Plan" before the next group session.

This Week's Plan

Work with your group leader each week to create a plan for personal study, worship, and application between sessions. Select from the following optional activities to match your personal preferences and available time.

Worship

[ ] Read your Bible. Complete the reading plan on page 20.

[ ] Spend time with God by engaging with the devotional experience on page 21.

[ ] Connect with God every day in prayer.

Personal Study

[ ] Read and interact with "You're a Saint!" on page 22.

[ ] Read and interact with "Don't Lose Your First Love" on page 26.

Application

[ ] Memorize Ephesians 1:2.

[ ] Identify an area of your life in which you need grace and peace.

[ ] Connect over coffee with someone in the group. Talk further through your thoughts on this week's study and your expectations for the group going forward.

[ ] Start a journal. This week record 10 things in which you've rooted your identity, other than Jesus, throughout your life. Based on the discussion in this week's group session, record 10 truths that would combat those false identities.

Did you miss the group session?
Video sessions available for purchase at *lifeway.com/ephesians*

19

Read

Read the following Scripture passages this week. Use the acronym HEAR and the space provided to record your thoughts or action steps.

Day 1: Ephesians 1

Day 2: Ephesians 2

Day 3: Ephesians 3

Day 4: Ephesians 4

Day 5: Ephesians 5

Day 6: Ephesians 6

Day 7: Ephesians 1–6

Reflect

TWO IDENTIFIABLE IDENTITY TRUTHS

Did you know you can buy identity-theft insurance? If someone steals your identity, you have a backup plan. You have security in knowing if your identity is stolen, you can recover your losses with minimal damage and can reclaim your lost identity.

Thankfully, our true identity in Christ is secure. Read these passages:

> To all who did receive him, to those who believed in his
> name, he gave the right to become children of God.
> **John 1:12**

> Accept one another, then, just as Christ accepted
> you, in order to bring praise to God.
> **Romans 15:7, NIV**

Notice two key truths about our identity from these verses:

1. When we receive Christ, we become children of God.
2. Our acceptance of others isn't contingent on their actions.
   It's contingent on Christ's acceptance of us.

As children of God, we receive all the family benefits: unconditional love, safety, provision, guidance, and much more. As brothers and sisters in Christ, we accept others regardless of how they've treated us, because God has loved us regardless of how we've treated Him. What amazing freedom is that?

Reflect on both of these truths. Which do you need to apply right now?

Personal Study 1

YOU'RE A SAINT!

Impersonating someone else is nothing new.

You may have discussed this fact in the group session. Kids dress up as superheroes, princesses, soldiers, monsters, or grown-ups. Imagination is fun, and imitation is natural.

There's a danger when we try to impersonate others' identities with our faith, though. Read these words from another of Paul's letters:

> I appeal to you, brothers, by the name of our Lord Jesus Christ, that all of you agree, and that there be no divisions among you, but that you be united in the same mind and the same judgment. For it has been reported to me by Chloe's people that there is quarreling among you, my brothers. What I mean is that each one of you says, "I follow Paul," or "I follow Apollos," or "I follow Cephas," or "I follow Christ."
> **1 Corinthians 1:10-12**

In this passage circle the activities Paul wants us to do.

Underline the dangers he's warning us against.

In Ephesians 1 Paul used a carefully chosen noun when he addressed the people to whom he wrote his letter. Check it out:

Paul, an apostle of Christ Jesus by the will of God,

To the saints who are in Ephesus, and are faithful in Christ Jesus.

Ephesians 1:1

While we're off somewhere trying to root our faith in the faith of others by identifying with a certain belief camp or "celebrity" preacher, Paul is calling us saints. Saints! Let that sink into your heart for a moment. (Also notice that Paul used the same word in 1:15,18; 3:8,18; 4:12; 5:3; 6:18.)

Be honest. When you think of a saint, who comes to mind?

What have they done or how did they live that caused you to record their name(s)?

Did you include yourself in that list? Why or why not?

The word *saint* finds its roots in the Old Testament, where God chose a people to be set apart from the other nations, to be His holy people. Now Christ has made us into His holy people (see Eph. 5:26). We're holy, not because of what we've done but because of what Christ has done. In other words, you're not a saint because you've lived a perfect life. You're a saint because Jesus did, and you've placed your faith in Him.

How does being a saint give you comfort and security?

What responsibilities do you feel that you have, now that you know you're a saint?

To be a saint means to be in Christ, or to be in union with Christ. The phrase "in Christ" occurs about 164 times in Paul's 13 epistles.[1] It's a central theme in Paul's writings, and it should be a central theme in our lives. We're united with Christ in His death as well as in His resurrection (see Eph. 2:5-7). To be in Christ doesn't mean we're inside Him. It means we're one with Him in the same way my arm is a part of my body. When we're in Christ, our desires are satisfied (see John 6:35), and we can rest eternally at peace, knowing we can't be snatched out of his hand (see John 10:28-30). We're protected. We're secure.

But one thing being in Christ doesn't give us is a lack of opposition. In fact, it may increase opposition. Though Satan can't destroy us, he would love nothing more than to destroy our sense of identity and intimacy with Christ. Temptation and pressure not to follow Christ closely can result in feeling disconnested, alone, and powerless in our spiritual walk.

Though we may be surrounded by opposition on every side, our eternal identity is secure:

> All that the Father gives me will come to me,
> and whoever comes to me I will never cast out.
> **John 6:37**

List ways you feel opposition even though you know your identity is secure.

List ways being united with Christ provides you with confidence to face opposition.

Close your study time in prayer, asking God to remind you of your sainthood every day.

I. Tony Merida, *Christ-Centered Exposition: Exalting Jesus in Ephesians* (Nashville: Holman Reference, 2014), 13.

Personal Study 2

DON'T LOSE YOUR FIRST LOVE

Paul's letter to the Ephesians isn't the only book of the Bible addressing that particular church. We read another account in Scripture about the people in Ephesus. Jesus had a word of correction and encouragement for them in the Book of Revelation:

> I know your works, your toil and your patient endurance, and how you cannot bear with those who are evil, but have tested those who call themselves apostles and are not, and found them to be false. I know you are enduring patiently and bearing up for my name's sake, and you have not grown weary. But I have this against you, that you have abandoned the love you had at first.
> **Revelation 2:2-4**

This passage identifies three qualities these people possessed that revealed a level of countercultural identity we don't often see today.

What positive traits were the Ephesians known for?

1.

2.

3.

Jesus said, "I know" (v. 2). What thoughts or feelings do you have when you read that Jesus was fully aware of everything—good and bad—in the Ephesians' lives?

What would you have done differently yesterday when you consider the fact that Jesus knows everything about your heart and actions?

As countercultural as the Ephesians' admirable qualities were, Jesus also had something against these people.

What did Jesus have against the Ephesians?

How would you describe the tone of Jesus' words *against* and *abandoned* in verse 4?

What was Jesus' point when He listed several positive qualities but identified one problem?

What does Jesus' emphasis reveal about the significance of love?

One of the saddest verses in all of Scripture is this: "You have abandoned the love you had at first" (v. 4). For people to have abandoned a first love means they once had a first love. They were in love with Jesus, but along the way their affections had shifted.

Let's take a married couple as an example. Let's assume their marriage of over a decade and their love for each other have never been stronger. They've had their share of bumps along the way, but in each season they've worked hard to intentionally love each other. The danger for them isn't that they'll randomly abandon each other one day. It's that their love will fade over time. If they cease intentionality in their marriage, their first love will slide into something much less. Even though on the outside everything may seem fine, when our hearts become disengaged, love begins to fade.

Our faith can do the same thing.

In your relationship with God, when have you abandoned your first love? What drew your heart away from Him?

In what parts of your life are you most prone to be motivated by anything other than the love of Christ?

Who in your life can help ensure that you don't slowly drift, backslide, or lose your genuine love for Christ?

Read Psalm 51.

Now look specifically at verses 10-12:

> Create in me a clean heart, O God,
>   and renew a right spirit within me.
> Cast me not away from your presence,
>   and take not your Holy Spirit from me.
> Restore to me the joy of your salvation,
>   and uphold me with a willing spirit.
> **Psalm 51:10-12**

Why did the psalmist need his joy to be restored?

What did he ask God to do to restore it?

When have you needed to ask God to restore your joy? How did He give you back the joy of His salvation?

It's possible for anyone to lose their love for Jesus. Rarely does it happen overnight, but over a series of events and seasons of life, our love can fade. When this happens, it's not the time to throw up our hands in exasperation. It's the time for spiritual renewal! The antidote for losing your love is to fall in love again.

Since you're just beginning this study, take the temperature of where you are in your relationship with God. Ask Him to meet you exactly where you are and to give you grace to grow as you fall more deeply in love with Him.

New Life in Christ

Knowing where we came from is important to understanding who we are, what we desire, and what makes us tick.

To understand our new identity, we've got to uncover our old identity. We've got to dig deeper into who we were, beyond our ancestry and family of origin, to see the ugly truth. Paul is going to show us an unfiltered picture of who we really are.

But light shines the brightest against a dark canvas. This week we're headed toward a beacon of bright, shining hope. This identity-shaping hope drives us toward action.

Ephesians 2:1-10 helps us clearly see three things:

1. What do we need to be saved from?

2. How are we saved?

3. What's the result of being saved?

The way you answer these questions will shape the way you live your life.

Start

Last week's reading plan suggested that you read one chapter of Ephesians each day. Was this anyone's first time to read through an entire book of the Bible? What was beneficial about reading the entire book?

What truths did God show you through the reading, reflection, or personal study this week? Which personal study ("You're a Saint!" or "Don't Lose Your First Love") resonated most deeply with you? Why?

How did you apply the truths to your life?

In this week's video Tony will walk us through Ephesians 2:1-10 as we learn who we were before we knew Jesus and the new life we're given through His death. We'll see some ways our identity is radically transformed through the greatest gift we've ever been given.

Pray that God will open your hearts and minds as you watch video session 2.

Watch

Use the space below to follow along and take notes as you watch video session 2.

Apart from Christ, we are spiritually _____.

We were _____ of God.

Jesus has become our substitute, and now we have _____.

This passage should compel us to _____. No one is beyond
the reach of God's amazing grace.

This text should encourage us to _____.

The text inspires us to _____. We want to work for the Savior.

Discuss

Use the following statements and questions to discuss the video.

More likely than not, you don't like to think of yourself as an enemy of God. But as Tony explained in teaching on Ephesians 2, that's exactly what we were before Jesus came into our lives.

Read Ephesians 2:1-3:

In this passage Paul used the phrase "among whom we all once lived ... like the rest of mankind" (v. 3). Nobody is exempt from the truth that apart from Christ, we're dead. Nobody.

Why is it significant that Paul referred to us as dead people?

Paul wasn't saying that before you knew Christ, you were as bad as you could be. You could have acted much worse than you did. You may have even done some good deeds! Paul was saying that without Christ as your King, without having been reborn with a new creature in Christ, your motives and actions couldn't ultimately please God (see Rom. 8:8) because you were cut off from the source of all life: God Himself. Dead things can't make themselves alive. So if we were dead, we need to be made alive.

Read Ephesians 2:4-7.

> God, being rich in mercy, because of the great love with which he
> loved us, even when we were dead in our trespasses, made us alive
> together with Christ—by grace you have been saved—and raised us
> up with him and seated us with him in the heavenly places in Christ
> Jesus, so that in the coming ages he might show the immeasurable
> riches of his grace in kindness toward us in Christ Jesus.
> **Ephesians 2:4-7**

Tony said, "Works matter to the Christian, but we're not working *for* salvation; we're working *from* salvation." The words *for* and *from* are subtle but incredibly important. The apostle Paul chose his words carefully.

If our works don't save us, then what purpose do they serve?

Read Ephesians 2:8-10.

Why is it vital to know that salvation is a gift, not a prize?

Tony walked through a short list of other religions, mentioning ways Christianity is different from all other world religions.

What makes Christianity distinct among all world religions and philosophies?

How would you explain the good news of the gospel?

It's important not only to know who you are in Christ but also to be able to share the good news of how Christ gave you a new identity.

1. Who were you before you came to know Christ?
2. How did you come to faith in Christ? Name two or three people who influenced you.
3. How are you different now? Name two or three events that have been significant in your spiritual life.

Conclude the group session with the prayer activity on the following page.

Pray

The good news of the gospel is that we were once dead, but God, in His grace and mercy, has made us alive in Christ. Take a couple of minutes to read and think about your answers to the following questions. Answer them on your own. Then share with the group if you're comfortable.

Whom do you know who needs to hear the good news? Write his or her name or initials here.

When are you going to see or communicate with them this week?

How will you share hope and truth with them?

Pray for two things:

1. One of your group members by name
2. The persons (or initials) members shared

To build accountability, reach out to the group member you're praying for this week. Check in to see how they're doing and to learn whether they've had a chance to talk with the person God placed on their heart.

Pray for the opportunities you'll each have and pray that God will open the hearts of people with whom we come in contact.

Prayer Requests

Encourage members to complete "This Week's Plan" before the next group session.

This Week's Plan

Worship

[ ] Read your Bible. Complete the reading plan on page 38.

[ ] Spend time with God by engaging with the devotional experience on page 39.

[ ] Connect with God every day in prayer.

Personal Study

[ ] Read and interact with "Dead Men Tell No Tales" on page 40.

[ ] Read and interact with "United with Christ" on page 44.

Application

[ ] Identify an area of your life that needs to change as a result of the truth you learned in this week's study.

[ ] Memorize Ephesians 2:8-9.

[ ] Connect over coffee with someone in the group. Talk further through your thoughts on this week's study and your expectations for the group going forward.

[ ] Continue your journal. This week record ways the truths of the gospel inform your daily life and ways you see God at work.

Did you miss the group session?
Video sessions available for purchase at *lifeway.com/ephesians*

37

Read

Read the following Scripture passages this week. Use the acronym HEAR and the space provided to record your thoughts or action steps.

Day 1: Ephesians 1:1-6

Day 2: Ephesians 1:7-14

Day 3: Ephesians 1:15-19

Day 4: Ephesians 1:20-23

Day 5: Ephesians 2:1-3

Day 6: Ephesians 2:4-10

Day 7: Ephesians 2:11-22

Reflect

WHO NEEDS RADICAL GRACE?

You were given radical grace. So radical that it raised dead things. Namely you.

Grace is something God gave to us that we didn't deserve and can't deserve. Read what Paul wrote to the Christians in Ephesus:

> God, being rich in mercy, because of the great love with which
> he loved us, even when we were dead in our trespasses, made
> us alive together with Christ—by grace you have been saved.
> **Ephesians 2:4-5**

God never gave up on you.

Not even when you were dead in sin.

He gave you salvation and new life in Christ.

So don't lose hope. Not on your circumstances. And not on other people. God is still in the business of bringing the dead to life.

What in your life feels dead or hopeless and needs God's radical grace to bring new life?

Record a short prayer to God, asking Him to do what only He can do.

Personal Study 1

DEAD MEN TELL NO TALES

Death is a topic we don't like to talk about. When we talk with others about death, we soften the language by using phrases like "passed away" and "no longer with us." Nobody likes going into a funeral home. The sights, colors, and smells stay with us long after we've left.

We don't like to talk about the death of anything. It's painful to talk about the death of a dream or the death of a relationship. We don't like it when our car dies; our refrigerator dies; or, God forbid, our phone dies.

When it comes to our spiritual lives, though, death is the way the Bible describes us apart from Jesus Christ.

Read what Paul wrote about spiritual death:

> To set the mind on the flesh is death, but to set the mind on
> the Spirit is life and peace. For the mind that is set on the flesh
> is hostile to God, for it does not submit to God's law; indeed,
> it cannot. Those who are in the flesh cannot please God.
> **Romans 8:6-8**

Apart from Christ we're dead. We can't even please God.

What does it to have a mind set on the flesh?

How do you think we can set our minds on the Spirit?

Renewing our minds is a supernatural act. There are activities we can and should do, but ultimately, we rely on the Holy Spirit to change our hearts and minds.

Read what Paul wrote about spiritual transformation in Romans 12:1-2.

> I appeal to you therefore, brothers, by the mercies of God, to present your bodies as a living sacrifice, holy and acceptable to God, which is your spiritual worship. Do not be conformed to this world, but be transformed by the renewal of your mind, that by testing you may discern what is the will of God, what is good and acceptable and perfect.
> **Romans 12:1-2**

"Living sacrifice" (v. I) is an oxymoron. It shouldn't be possible. A sacrifice is something that has died and is being presented as an offering. Yet this is precisely how Paul described us.

If a "living sacrifice" is "your spiritual worship" (v. I), how would you describe worship? Record a definition in your own words.

The words *conformed* and *transformed* are contrasting terms. To be conformed is a passive state in which people, circumstances, and seasons of life are conforming you to themselves. To be transformed is to be changed, and this comes through a renewed mind. It's the difference between going downhill (conformed) and going uphill (transformed). Another way to think about it is that it's the difference between swimming with the current (conformed) and swimming against the current (transformed). In our flesh we naturally drift toward conformity. But when we're united with Christ, we're being transformed.

What time in your life did you feel yourself conforming to life around you? What was that like?

What time in your life did you feel yourself being transformed by Christ? What was that like?

According to this passage, we learn God's will for our lives by testing it (see v. 2). Sometimes this happens individually. Sometimes this happens in community as others who love us and want God's best for our lives confirm or deny God's leading in our lives.

If you want to know God's will for your life, how will you be intentional this week to test and discern what's good?

Transformation is possible. By God's grace we can be transformed from death to life. Our lives can become acts of worship as living sacrifices. We can wage war against the self-destructive desires of our flesh and set our minds on the goodness of our Heavenly Father.

Read Jesus' parable of the prodigal son in Luke 15:11-32.

How did the father's reaction to his son's return compare to the way you think of God?

The older brother was bitter and frustrated because although he didn't rebel against his father, his brother was thrown a party after rebelling and returning home.

What was so wrong about the older brother's reaction?

When have you found yourself acting like the older brother?

Read Ephesians 2:1-5.

John Newton wrote these words in the late 1700s:

> Amazing grace! how sweet the sound
> That saved a wretch like me!
> I once was lost but now am found,
> Was blind, but now I see.[1]

Looking back on your life, when have you been most thankful for grace?

As you close in prayer, worship God. Praise Him for the life you have and the escape from death He provided through Jesus.

I. John Newton, "Amazing Grace! How Sweet the Sound," in *Baptist Hymnal* (Nashville: LifeWay Worship, 2008), 104.

Personal Study 2

UNITED WITH CHRIST

To be united with Christ means we're one with Him. Obviously, this should result in a changed life. If we're united with Christ in His death, burial, and resurrection, our lives should show evidence of that union.

In the previous study we focused on God's amazing, transforming grace. There's nothing we could do to bring ourselves from death to life. Our salvation isn't the result of our own works, but works are a part of the Christian life as a child of God:

> By grace you have been saved through faith. And this is not your own doing; it is the gift of God, not a result of works, so that no one may boast. For we are his workmanship, created in Christ Jesus for good works, which God prepared beforehand, that we should walk in them.
> **Ephesians 2:8-10**

The Bible calls our changed life and the new actions that result fruit. Paul went into more detail about what this fruit looks like in his letter to the church in Galatia:

> The fruit of the Spirit is love, joy, peace, patience, kindness, goodness, faithfulness, gentleness, self-control; against such things there is no law.
> **Galatians 5:22-23**

Notice the singular word: *fruit*. Not *fruits*. This is significant because when we're united with Christ, the work of the Spirit should manifest itself in all of these ways in our lives. We don't get to say, "I'm kind; that's my fruit. But I'm not patient; I don't have that fruit." If you're in Christ, you have all of this fruit.

Which characteristic(s) in these verses are easiest for you to express?

Which are the most difficult?

Why do you think some are more difficult for you to live out?

Although we're in Christ, we're also still living in our mortal bodies. Which means we mess up and sin much more than we would ever like.

Maybe there's something you did that you regret. Someone you hurt. Somewhere you went. Someone you trusted. You were hurt by someone.

Maybe your mistakes were made public, putting your life on display as a spectacle for others. Maybe someone else's stupid decisions affected you. And you'd like your mulligan to cancel out that person's choices too.

What have you done that you're ashamed of?

To whom have you confessed that?

The good news about being in Christ is that when we repent and confess our sin, God removes our guilt and shame.

Read Psalm 103:8-12.

> The LORD is merciful and gracious,
>   slow to anger and abounding in steadfast love.
> He will not always chide,
>   nor will he keep his anger forever.
> He does not deal with us according to our sins,
>   nor repay us according to our iniquities.
> For as high as the heavens are above the earth,
>   so great is his steadfast love toward those who fear him;
> as far as the east is from the west,
>   so far does he remove our transgressions from us.
> **Psalm 103:8-12**

Circle the character traits of God that you see in this psalm.

Which of these traits do you need most right now? Why?

Do you know how far the east is from the west? Infinite. Because the east and the west never touch. Ever. East is never west, and west is never east. "As far as the east is from the west" (v. 12) means God has completely removed your sin from you.

As you reflect on the painful choices you've made in life, how does knowing that God doesn't hold them against you make you feel?

To whom do you need to extend that same type of mercy?

David went on to say about God:

> As a father shows compassion to his children,
>> so the LORD shows compassion to those who fear him.
> **Psalm 103:13**

A father doesn't hate his children who need a redo. He has compassion for them. We may hold on to our hurt, our despair, and our frustrations. We may cling to our past failures. But God offers "steadfast love" (v. 11) to us. He "redeems your life from the pit" (v. 4) In fact, the moment we turn to God, we find Him running to us, as the father ran to welcome the prodigal son home. He's not standing there with His arms crossed, ready to condemn us. Through Christ He has removed our sins from us.

To be united with Christ means we get to receive the glorious gift of compassion.

As you close this week's personal study, thank God that He's removed your sins from you. Ask Him to give you strength to live life not as someone who's bound by guilt but as a child of God who walks in freedom.

New Life in Community

Week 3

We all long to belong. Feeling left out cuts us to our core because something deep inside us wants to be known, accepted, and loved. And this isn't a bad thing! In fact, it's a God-given desire to be part of a community of people that accepts us for who He created us to be.

This week's Scripture focuses on our pre-Christ alienated state. As in previous weeks, we'll learn that we can't fully embrace the good until we lock eyes with the bad. Again as in previous weeks, we'll notice that our pre-Christ state is pretty bleak.

But Paul shows us that Christ's death was sufficient to reconcile us to one another, forming a community of people to whom we now belong.

If you've ever wished you were part of a group you weren't invited to, if you've ever felt on the outside, this week's study will show you once and for all that Jesus died to fulfill your craving to belong by making us citizens of a new kingdom.

But living in community isn't going to be easy. Anytime you bring sinners into proximity with sinners, challenges crop up. Let's see what Ephesians 2 has to say about overcoming this reality to build healthy communities.

Start

What truths did you discover through the reading, reflection, or personal study this week? How did you apply the truths to your life?

From the personal study "United with Christ," which fruit did you struggle to exhibit this week? How did you see growth?

We've learned the truth that Jesus died to reconcile us to God, and this week we'll dive into the truth that Jesus also died to reconcile us to others. As important as it is for us to live at peace with God (our vertical relationship), it's vital for us to live at peace with others (our horizontal relationships). If that challenges you already, then good! Here we go!

Pray that God will open your hearts and minds as you watch video session 3.

Watch

Use the space below to follow along and take notes as you watch video session 3.

It's the gospel that brings _____ groups of people together.

If you're in Christ, not only do you have a new _____. You have a new _____.

We have a new _____.

We have new brothers and sisters. We are made part of the _____ of God.

You're _____ of the kingdom of God.

We're a _____.

Discuss

When we think about rivalries, it's easy to think of sports teams or political parties. It's easy not only because they come to mind quickly but also because they tend to operate outside us. We don't have to look our rival in the eye every week. It becomes more personal when your rival is sitting across the room from you.

Have you ever met a difficult person? What made them so difficult?

Read Ephesians 2:11-12.

Paul described us as "separated from Christ, alienated" (v. 12). What does it mean to be alienated from others?

From whom do you feel alienated at this time in your life?

What would reconciliation look like for you?

In verses 11-12 Paul tells us that we were apart from Christ, separated from God, and without hope. It's really a bleak picture. But the Paul described an amazing change.

Read Ephesians 2:13-14.

Christ's blood is the bridge that brings us near, though we were once far off.

What's significant about "the blood of Christ" (v. 13)?

Based on these verses, what should we do when there's a wall between us and someone else?

Read Ephesians 2:19-22.

The apostle Paul shared three pictures of the community we become part of when we're reconciled to one another.

> **Which of these pictures do you need the most in your life right now? Why?**

> **How would you respond to someone who says, "I love Jesus, but I don't love His church"?**

Being reconciled with God doesn't mean that working in unity with people is easy. But even though it's not easy to live in unity with other believers, Jesus died to bring us together. So it must be important!

Jesus died for His church. That's all of us—you, me, people who are different from us, and even people who are legitimately hard to get along with.

> **What relationship is strained or broken in your life, especially a relationship with another Christian?**

> **Share that information with the person on your left. (Use initials or describe the situation if you aren't comfortable sharing the name.)**

Here are a few action steps you could take this week.

1. Pray for that person.
2. Ask God to soften your heart toward them.
3. Call the person.
4. Write the person a note, an email, or a text.
5. Have a face-to-face meeting.

Conclude the group session with the prayer activity on the following page.

Pray

A step of faith in the right direction is worth celebrating. Whatever your step is, whether big or small, be courageous and take it this week.

Remind yourself of the following three things.

1. The grace God has shown to you through Christ

2. The grace God has made available to all people

3. The broken relationship whose unity you identified as being difficult to maintain in your own efforts

Take a few moments to reflect silently on these verses:

> Now in Christ Jesus you who once were far off have been brought near by the blood of Christ. For he himself is our peace, who has made us both one and has broken down in his flesh the dividing wall of hostility.
> **Ephesians 2:13-14**

As you close in prayer, have each person say a prayer aloud for the person on the right and for the person with whom they need to pursue a relationship.

Prayer Requests

Encourage members to complete "This Week's Plan" before the next group session.

This Week's Plan

Worship

[ ] Read your Bible. Complete the reading plan on page 56.

[ ] Spend time with God by engaging with the devotional experience on page 57.

[ ] Connect with God every day in prayer.

Personal Study

[ ] Read and interact with "Is Community Really That Important?" on page 58.

[ ] Read and interact with "Diversity Is Essential" on page 62.

Application

[ ] Identify an area of your life that needs to change as a result of the truth you learned in this week's study.

[ ] Memorize Ephesians 2:13.

[ ] Connect over coffee with someone in the group. Talk with them through some difficulties you are having or have had in relationships. Be vulnerable.

[ ] Continue your journal. This week record the many ways God has been patient and kind with you. Make a list of people who haven't earned but definitely need your grace and love.

Did you miss the group session?
Video sessions available for purchase at *lifeway.com/ephesians*

55

Read

Read the following Scripture passages this week. Use the acronym HEAR and the space provided to record your thoughts or action steps.

Day 1: Ephesians 2:11-16

Day 2: Ephesians 2:17-22

Day 3: Ephesians 3:1-7

Day 4: Ephesians 3:8-12

Day 5: Ephesians 3:13-19

Day 6: Ephesians 3:20-21

Day 7: Ephesians 4

Reflect

ANSWERING WITH OUR ACTIONS

Did you know one of the most beautiful marks of faith is loving other people? It is! Jesus said this:

> By this all people will know that you are my
> disciples, if you have love for one another.
> **John 13:35**

The answer to this question isn't found simply in contemplation. It's found in doing. Loving other people gives evidence to a lost world that we're followers of Christ.

Christian love is a no-matter-what kind of commitment. It's an unbreakable bond in our shared love of Jesus. It's a peace that transcends all things. No differences or conflicts should divide God's church. The closer we walk with Christ, the closer we walk with one another. Paul described this kind of love this way:

> Now in Christ Jesus you who once were far off have been brought near
> by the blood of Christ. For he himself is our peace, who has made us
> both one and has broken down in his flesh the dividing wall of hostility.
> **Ephesians 2:13-14**

Remember today that Christ died not only for your sins but also for those of the people around you. When you begin to see others as being loved by God, your heart changes. You realize that nothing should come between us. No matter what happens, choose to show love rather than allowing anything to become a barrier in your relationship—a barrier that makes it hard for the world around you to see that you're Christ's disciple.

Personal Study 1

IS COMMUNITY REALLY THAT IMPORTANT?

Does church matter? Does a small group matter? You may have asked yourself these questions. In fact, you may be asking them right now, three weeks into this study. Is it really worth the effort to engage in others' lives?

But church isn't a place; it's a people. It's not a building; it's a body. This idea may not be surprising to you today, but in the time when Paul wrote the Book of Ephesians, it was a radical shift in religious culture. The temple in Jerusalem was central to the identity of the Jewish people. Not only was it a place of worship, but it was also seen as the place where God dwelled. Paul applied Jewish beliefs about the temple to the body of Christ:

> You are no longer strangers and aliens, but you are fellow citizens with the saints and members of the household of God, built on the foundation of the apostles and prophets, Christ Jesus himself being the cornerstone, in whom the whole structure, being joined together, grows into a holy temple in the Lord. In him you also are being built together into a dwelling place for God by the Spirit.
> **Ephesians 2:19-22**

The Early Church

What does it look like to live as God's dwelling place, filled with the Spirit and united in Jesus? Let's start by looking at the New Testament church as it was in its infancy stages. The Book of Acts is the story of the birth and rapid growth, of the church. Acts 2 is a key chapter that gives us a picture of the church as it operated in two primary delivery systems: in the temple courts and from house to house.

In Acts 2:14-41 Peter publicly preached the first Christian sermon, and three thousand people were saved in one day. Acts 2:42-47 shows the rhythm of daily life in the early church.

Read Acts 2:42-47.

They devoted themselves to the apostles' teaching and the fellowship,
to the breaking of bread and the prayers. And awe came upon every soul,
and many wonders and signs were being done through the apostles. And
all who believed were together and had all things in common. And they
were selling their possessions and belongings and distributing the proceeds
to all, as any had need. And day by day, attending the temple together
and breaking bread in their homes, they received their food with glad and
generous hearts, praising God and having favor with all the people. And
the Lord added to their number day by day those who were being saved.
Acts 2:42-47

On a scale of 1 to 10, how would you rate your commitment
to Christian community?

1   2   3   4   5   6   7   8   9   10

Not at all   Wholeheartedly

Identify ways you're intentional about nurturing each of the
following characteristics used to describe the early church.

Bible study (the apostles' teaching):

Fellowship:

Worship (breaking of bread, attending the temple):

Prayer:

Generosity (having all things in common):

Hospitality (gathering in homes):

Which one of the blessings of living in community excites you most in this season of your life? Why?

Living Life in Community

Let's look at another passage to see some more practical aspects of our relationships within Christian community.

Read 1 Thessalonians 5:14.

> We urge you, brothers, admonish the idle, encourage
> the fainthearted, help the weak, be patient with them all.
> **1 Thessalonians 5:14**

Paul was writing to the church in Thessalonica, but he was also writing to us. We're the brothers he mentioned.

Identify times when someone has done these things for you.

Admonish:

Encourage:

Help:

Be patient:

Now go back through the list of actions, identifying other people who need you to come alongside them in each of these ways.

None of these activities can be done well alone. In fact, they can't even be done in brief passing. It's not possible to admonish the idle (in an authentic way) in a brief-passing conversation. You must be in a relationship with them to even know they're idle. The same goes for someone who is faint-hearted, is weak, or needs patience. The command Paul gave here implies a life lived in community, not one lived in isolation.

Day by Day

Community is something we should be afraid to walk away from. Did you know if you're living your faith in isolation, you're in danger?

Read Hebrews 3:12-13.

This is one of the most frightening verses in Scripture. Although our identities in Christ are eternally secure, never forget that our hearts are still vulnerable. We need one another because sin chips little pieces of our hearts away bit by bit. Rarely are we drawn away from God in an instant by huge bites. However, there's the real chance that sin can deceive us and draw our hearts away, and we would never even know it. Our hearts can grow callous toward God's activity in the people around us before we realize it.

> **Honestly, in what ways do you need to be held accountable? Whom will you ask to encourage you in your spiritual walk and to help you guard against the deceitfulness of sin?**

God intends for His people to live in relationship with one another; this has been the plan since He created man and woman. It isn't good for us to be alone. We need helpers (see Gen. 2:18). There's not only great joy but also great protection in community.

Personal Study 2

DIVERSITY IS ESSENTIAL

If Jesus' death on the cross was truly intended to bring reconciliation vertically (our relationship with God) and horizontally with all people, shouldn't our churches be the most diverse communities on the planet? We were all aliens who "have been brought near by the blood of Christ" (Eph. 2:13). This passage doesn't just refer to soccer moms or athletes or engineers. It doesn't just refer to Americans coming together with Americans. We were all aliens. Every race, tribe, and tongue needed to be reconciled to one another. That's the picture John gave us in Revelation:

> After this I looked, and behold, a great multitude that no one could number, from every nation, from all tribes and peoples and languages, standing before the throne and before the Lamb, clothed in white robes, with palm branches in their hands, and crying out with a loud voice, "Salvation belongs to our God who sits on the throne, and to the Lamb!"
> **Revelation 7:9-10**

Be honest. On a scale from 1 to 10, how diverse is your church?

1   2   3   4   5   6   7   8   9   10

No diversity   Every tribe, tongue, and nation

Why did you pick the number you picked?

What would it take to increase that number?

Before we shift the blame to others, let's check our own hearts for signs of favoritism. We all gravitate toward people we find comfortable. For some of us, it's a money matter. Whether or not you say it, you view the poor with disdain. Or you view the rich with disdain. Or the skinny. Or the overweight. Others of us gravitate toward a certain people group. Or away from those who don't look like us.

What types of people do you try to avoid when they enter the room?

Read James 2:8-13.

This passage gives us great insight into the danger of showing partiality. It also gives us the remedy.

What does it mean to "love your neighbor as yourself" (v. 8)?

When have you struggled to live up to that definition?

Would you rather be judged with mercy or without mercy?

The moment we show favoritism to someone because of the color of their skin, the money in their pocket, or the shoes on their feet is the moment we break "the royal law" (v. 8).

You might be tempted to throw up your hands in the air and say, "Our church is so far from being diverse, there's nothing I can do!" It's actually quite simple, but that doesn't mean it's easy. Look at what Scripture says.

> Above all, keep loving one another earnestly, since love covers a multitude of sins. Show hospitality to one another without grumbling. As each has received a gift, use it to serve one another, as good stewards of God's varied grace.
> **1 Peter 4:8-10**

There's an implied statement in the phrase "without grumbling" (v. 9). The implication is that you probably have good reason to grumble. After all, when you show hospitality, people eat your food, drink your drinks, and make a mess of your house. Showing hospitality to others is expensive, costing you precious resources, finances, time, and emotion.

When was the last time you showed hospitality to someone who couldn't show hospitality to you in return?

List the names of five people from different backgrounds whom you could invite into your home.

1.

2.

3.

4.

5.

You can't possibly change everything in the world. But when you're hospitable toward others, especially others who are different from you, you show the world that you serve a God who loves all people.

Don't let hospitality stop at the threshold of your house. Invite people from different ethnic backgrounds to your church's worship service. Advocate for disenfranchised people groups. Care for orphans from other people groups. The more we do these things, the more we bring the kingdom of God to earth, and the more we prepare our hearts for heaven.

Ultimately, we have one Father. We're brothers and sisters in Christ, "members of the household of God" (Eph. 2:19). The church is one big, beautiful, diverse family.

In the middle of his letter to the Christians in Ephesus, Paul seemed to become overwhelmed by this incredible reality. He paused to praise God for a love that transforms us from the inside out and to pray for the strength to live as a holy community of faith in this world.

Use Paul's prayer below to praise God for the body of Christ.

For this reason I bow my knees before the Father, from whom every family in heaven and on earth is named, that according to the riches of his glory he may grant you to be strengthened with power through his Spirit in your inner being, so that Christ may dwell in your hearts through faith—that you, being rooted and grounded in love, may have strength to comprehend with all the saints what is the breadth and length and height and depth, and to know the love of Christ that surpasses knowledge, that you may be filled with all the fullness of God. Now to him who is able to do far more abundantly than all that we ask or think, according to the power at work within us, to him be glory in the church and in Christ Jesus throughout all generations, forever and ever. Amen.
Ephesians 3:14-21

Pursuing Unity in Christ

Week 4

Unity is one of the most difficult states to pursue. Because our agendas never line up exactly, someone always has to set aside his or her own desire to unite with another person or group.

To pursue unity together, each person needs to choose humility. It's a two-way street, contingent on the Holy Spirit's work in each of our lives. Part of Christian unity is intentionally allowing love to win instead of secondary theological, philosophical, and political agendas.

When we live together in unity, we function as one unit or body. A healthy body is a unified body. Each body part contributes its specified function, doing its specified duty, to serve the collective whole.

When our churches bicker and complain against one another, we show ourselves to be no different from our culture. But when our churches function together in unity, we paint a picture to the world of a good God who loves His people. A unified church is attractive to a lost world.

Ephesians 4 will teach us what a healthy, unified church looks like.

Start

We've just crossed the halfway mark in this study of Ephesians.

What's something new you've learned so far?

What has really challenged your faith?

How has studying Ephesians had practical application for you?

As you completed your personal study of week 3, what did you learn about the value of community?

How did God use last week's memory verse, Ephesians 2:13, in your life this week?

In Ephesians 2 we saw that God gives us new life in Christ and, beginning in verse II, that our new identity leads us into a new community. Ephesians 4 will teach us how we're to live in this new community called the church.

Pray that God will open your hearts and minds as you watch video session 4.

Watch

Use the space below to follow along and take notes as you watch video session 4.

The church is a _____.

A healthy church is marked by spiritual _____.

We're united by _____, _____, and a common _____.

This is a _____ to be part of the body of Christ.

A healthy church is marked by spiritual _____.

If you're _____ spiritually, it's not for your benefit. It's for the benefit of the church.

A healthy church is marked by a growing _____.

What happens when you have a _____ in the church? You can fight, you can flee, or you can follow Ephesians 4.

Discuss

As we continue our discussion of unity, think about the context of your local church.

> What evidence have you seen that your church is characterized by a supernatural unity?

> What action steps have you personally taken to fight against disunity?

Read Ephesians 4:1-3.

> How would you define the characteristics Paul used to describe the Christian life—humility, gentleness, patience, and love?

> What's the opposite of each of those qualities?

> How have you seen each of these contributing to or detracting from eagerly maintaining "the unity of the Spirit in the bond of peace" (v. 3)?

People don't drift toward unity but away from it. Part of maintaining unity sometimes means having difficult conversations. God often shows up in these awkward conversations as we're trying to reconcile differences. It shouldn't surprise us, because Jesus cares about the unity of His church.

> When was the last time you maintained unity by having a difficult conversation with someone?

> Knowing what you know about the value of unity for the health of your church, how would you begin a difficult conversation now?

Tony highlights the three main elements that unite us:

1. Character (see v. 2)

2. Calling (see v. 4)

3. Confession (see vv. 4-6)

How have you seen these elements build unity among Christians?

How have you seen damaging effects in relationships and specifically in a church when any of these three areas are neglected?

Tony said in the video:

> Some people say, "I don't see any need for a church. I don't see how the church is going to bless me." That's wrongheaded thinking, so I flip it on them and say, "Have you ever thought that the church needs you and your spiritual gifts?"

How would you use a story from your life to help someone who says they don't need church see the mutual benefit of community?

Read Ephesians 4:11-13.

How have you used your spiritual gifts in the church?

In what ways does diversity benefit the church?

Conclude the group session with the prayer activity on the following page.

Pray

We talked about using our spiritual gifts to build up the body of Christ. Record a couple of different ways you can serve your church with the spiritual gifts that God has given you.

We also talked about four qualities required to maintain unity among believers:

1. Humility
2. Gentleness
3. Patience
4. Love

Circle the quality you most need to work on.

Divide into same-gender groups of two or three and identify the quality you need to work on. If you're comfortable, pray aloud for one other person in the group. Ask God to identify specific, creative, unique ways they can use their gifts to strengthen your small group and your local church.

Prayer Requests

Encourage members to complete "This Week's Plan" before the next group session.

This Week's Plan

Worship

[ ] Read your Bible. Complete the reading plan on page 74.

[ ] Spend time with God by engaging with the devotional experience on page 75.

[ ] Connect with God every day in prayer.

Personal Study

[ ] Read and interact with "Unity or Uniformity?" on page 76.

[ ] Read and interact with "Knowledge and Love" on page 80.

Application

[ ] Identify an area of your life that needs to change as a result of the truth you learned in this week's study.

[ ] Memorize Ephesians 4:1-3.

[ ] Connect over coffee with someone in the group. Share with them a spiritual gift you see in them. Ask them to share gifts they see in you.

[ ] Continue your journal. This week record ways you can work to live in harmony with others in your local church. Identify some ways you can do this well and some ways you've caused discord in the past.

Did you miss the group session?
Video sessions available for purchase at *lifeway.com/ephesians*

73

Read

Read the following Scripture passages this week. Use the acronym HEAR and the space provided to record your thoughts or action steps.

Day 1: Ephesians 4:1-3

Day 2: Ephesians 4:4-6

Day 3: Ephesians 4:7-13

Day 4: Ephesians 4:14-16

Day 5: Ephesians 4:17-24

Day 6: Ephesians 4:25-32

Day 7: Ephesians 5

Reflect

YOU GET A SUPERPOWER, AND YOU GET A SUPERPOWER, AND YOU GET A SUPERPOWER ...

You know you have a superpower, right? You—yes, you—have been given a spiritual gift, a supernatural power. Check out I Corinthians 12:8-10; Romans 12:6-8; and Ephesians 4:11-13 to get an idea of some of the gifts God has given us. Did you realize, though, that the spiritual gift you've been given isn't really for you? First Peter 4:10 says, "As each has received a gift, use it to serve one another, as good stewards of God's varied grace."

First Corinthians 12:7 says, "To each is given the manifestation of the Spirit for the common good." Our gifts collectively make up the body of Christ. This means if you don't exercise your spiritual gift, not only do you lose out on the joy of expressing your God-given gift, but we all lose out because our body isn't complete. We can identify two truths about our gifts in this passage:

1. Our spiritual gifts are manifestations of the Holy Spirit. So if you don't exercise your gifts, the Holy Spirit isn't made present through you to others. That's a lot of responsibility!
2. Your spiritual gift is designed "for the common good," which means if you don't exercise the Holy Spirit, good of the body isn't as good as it could be.

Which of the previous responsibilities resonates most deeply with you? Why?

This week as you reflect on the spiritual gifts God has given you, consider ways you can use those gifts to bless and serve others.

Personal Study 1

UNITY OR UNIFORMITY?

As you think about the concept of unity, be careful not to equate unity with uniformity. These are different concepts. *Unity* means we're working at peace, together with one another. *Uniformity* means we're working to become the same person, clones of one another, losing our unique identity. Consider what Paul wrote to the Ephesians:

> [God] gave the apostles, the prophets, the evangelists, the shepherds and teachers, to equip the saints for the work of ministry, for building up the body of Christ, until we all attain to the unity of the faith and of the knowledge of the Son of God, to mature manhood, to the measure of the stature of the fullness of Christ.
> **Ephesians 4:11-13**

Paul made clear to the Ephesians that God doesn't expect or desire uniformity. He gave different people different abilities. We're each unique. Each of these unique gifts is for the same purpose—unity. We're called to pursue unity, not uniformity. We do that in three primary ways.

In Our Gifting

Our giftings are unique. They're supernatural gifts from God that are given to us to serve others. They're influenced by our past hurts and failures, our successes, our parents, and our influences. They're shaped by where we live and the environments God has allowed us to walk through. They're molded by our personalities.

Your gifting is unique to you. I see the value of a gift like administration, but I sure don't have it! If I could force you to look just like me and have my gifts, we would become a church with a huge arm but no legs. Or we would become a church with a massive nose but no chin. Eww.

We tend to look at others' gifts, though, and wish they were ours. You wish you were better at teaching than she is. You wish you were better at hospitality, as he is. But if we all don't express our gifts, our whole church loses.

Read 1 Corinthians 12:22-25.

In our human economy we think the most important gifts are the ones that are seen publicly. But Paul pointed out that "those parts of the body that we think less honorable we bestow the greater honor" (v. 23). He flipped our scale on its head.

How have you used your spiritual gifts to serve others in the past month?

Do you have spiritual gifts that aren't noticed or seem insignificant? Based on 1 Corinthians 12:22-25, why is your gifting valuable to the body of Christ?

When you try to conform your gifts to match someone else's, we all lose. Your gifts go unexpressed, and our body of believers becomes weaker. Live in unity, not uniformity.

Over Nonessentials

Read 1 Corinthians 3:3-9.

The question is not whether we have problems in our church. The question is how we can contribute to the unity of our church. We don't contribute to unity by fighting with one another. In the passage we read, Paul said we're acting in the flesh when we're jealous and full of strife.

It's easy to disagree with someone and dismiss them because of their beliefs. That's what was going on in the Corinthian church. Individuals were uniting themselves with the teachings of various leaders and were disagreeing with anyone who thought differently.

It's not wrong to disagree with someone, especially over secondary issues. But recognizing which issues are primary and which are secondary is important when it comes to unity (see Eph. 4:4-6 for the primary theological ideas). But it's not healthy to divide over secondary issues and claim allegiance to a certain teacher over allegiance to God.

What kinds of issues are secondary? Any the Bible hasn't clearly spoken on.

Over what issues have you seen relationships fracture that the Bible hasn't clearly spoken on?

Has there been a time in your life where someone put their preferences aside for the sake of loving you?

Uniformity says, "We all have to believe exactly the same thing about every single Scripture in order to have fellowship together."

Unity says, "I love you enough to disagree but maintain fellowship."

What secondary issues are often elevated to a place of primary importance, causing division among Christians?

When We're Sinned Against

What should we do when we're sinned against? Uniformity would say, "We just all need to agree, even when one person was hurt." Unity says, "Our relationship is broken, and I love you enough to work to restore what we lost."

Read Matthew 18:15-20.

When was a time you restored unity in the way Jesus lays taught in this passage?

The opposite of the Matthew 18 approach would be to gossip about a person instead of going to them directly.

When have you seen gossip break down unity?

What should you do to stop a gossip train?

So the question is, Are you going to let your secondary-issue agenda win? Or are you going to put on the virtues of Christ, maintain unity, and have the difficult conversations necessary for the good of the church and the glory of God?

Personal Study 2

KNOWLEDGE AND LOVE

In Ephesians 4 we learn that we should no longer be:

> … children, tossed to and fro by the waves and carried about by every
> wind of doctrine, by human cunning, by craftiness in deceitful schemes.
> **Ephesians 4:14**

As we grow up in our faith, it's important that we grow in our understanding of sound biblical doctrine. Otherwise, as Paul said here, we're prone to being tossed around with every doctrinal and theological fad that comes along.

But there are proper and improper applications of this verse. Let's look at another time that Paul wrote about being a child.

Read 1 Corinthians 13, paying special attention to verse 11 below.

> When I was a child, I spoke like a child, I thought like a child, I reasoned
> like a child. When I became a man, I gave up childish ways.
> **1 Corinthians 13:11**

Imagine a two-year-old kid. She speaks, thinks, and reasons like a child. If you could sum all that up in one phrase, it would be this: "It's all about me!" Everything she does is about meeting her own desires. And if you get in the way of her pursuit, she'll let you know.

In I Corinthians 13 Paul equated maturity with love. To give up childish ways means to pursue love, not just our self-interest. As important as it is to learn sound doctrine, we should never sacrifice the application of that doctrine. It's the difference between head knowledge and heart knowledge.

Think of someone you know who has been consumed by their pursuit of knowledge. How did being around them make you feel?

Babies are cute. We love to hold them, hear them make baby noises, give them bottles, and watch them roll around. But those same noises, behaviors, and actions aren't so cute when a baby turns into an adult. If you walked into someone's home and the dad was cooing in his crib while gazing at a spinning mobile, you would be right to think something was wrong.

In a similar way, when you become a Christian, you're a baby. And that's good! Babies do baby things. But you aren't intended to stay that way. You need to learn and grow as a believer.

What are some of the most important doctrines a new believer should understand and apply?

What are some of the most important behaviors a maturing believer should practice?

In what ways are you prone to exhibit an immature faith?

If I ... understand all mysteries and all knowledge, ...

but have not love, I am nothing.

1 Corinthians 13:2

Can you imagine if you could understand all mysteries and all knowledge? How powerful would you be? How historic would you be? How ... unbearable would you be? You would never be wrong! Love may not give us power or write our names in history books, but it gives us what other people value. It's the proper application of knowledge.

Be honest. Can you recount a time when you participated in an "I'm right and you're wrong" argument?

In that situation how could you have let love win?

In another passage in I Corinthians, Paul wrote, " 'Knowledge' puffs up, but love builds up" (I Cor. 8:I). Knowledge can make you look good and feel good. Have you ever heard the phrase "He's got a big head"? Someone gets a big head because they increase in knowledge (usually about themselves) without increasing in love.

As we begin following Christ, our knowledge about ourselves increases vastly. The Bible even calls us saints. Knowledge alone builds us up, but it's not guaranteed to build others up (at least not in and of itself). It may build you up, but that's where it stops. Love, however, makes the whole body stronger.

What are some major points of knowledge you've gained so far in this study?

Can you come up with a few practical ways love can flow out of your knowledge? Record them below.

As we respond to Paul's warning in Ephesians 4:14 not to be tossed around "by every wind of doctrine," let's also practice Ephesians 4:15 to live out truth and love:

Rather, speaking the truth in love, we are to grow up in every way into him who is the head, into Christ.
Ephesians 4:15

Pursuing Holiness in Christ

in Christ

Week 5

Do you ever hear the ice-cream truck blaring its horn through your neighborhood? It brings back childhood memories of standing in the road staring at the side of the ice-cream truck, trying to decide between an ice-cream sandwich, a chocolate-vanilla combo served in the shape of a cartoon character, with a cold, stale piece of bubble gum waiting for you at the end. Ah … nostalgia.

As children, ice-cream trucks were almost magical. As adults, though, the distorted horn sounds like the music from a horror movie. It makes you wonder why you ever thought buying ice cream from the busted window of a stranger's rusty van was magical.

As we grow up, our perspectives change. We start to see a picture that's bigger than what we think we want in any given moment. Sometimes, though, we slip back into childish ways, reaching for ice cream from a rusty van.

We should all hope that, as time progresses, we find ourselves growing closer to the Lord. Our walk with Christ should continue to become more intimate through progressive sanctification as we seek to put off our old self—our former way of life—and put on our new self that has been created to be like God, full of holiness (see Eph. 4:22-24).

This week we're going to take a look at holiness and its practical implications for our Christian lives.

Start

Last week we talked about spiritual gifts and learned that we each have been gifted to serve and build up the body of Christ, the church. If each of us doesn't express our supernatural gifts, we suffer individually and corporately.

What did you learn about the difference between unity and uniformity?

How did you apply the truths from the personal study "Knowledge and Love" in the following areas of your life?

Home:

Work:

School:

Neighborhood:

This week we'll examine holiness and its implications for our daily lives. How do we pursue holiness? What should we do when we fail? What kinds of behaviors and attitudes should characterize God's people who are pursuing holiness?

Pray that God will open your hearts and minds as you watch video session 5.

Watch

Use the space below to follow along and take notes as you watch video session 5.

Positionally, we're _____. We are _____. We've been declared righteous. This is all because of the work of Christ.

_____ and holiness are not at odds. They go together.

God's _____ for our lives involves the pursuit of holiness.

Walk in _____, _____, and _____.

Love involves compassion that leads to _____.

The Christian is not just to _____ darkness. We are to _____ darkness as well.

We walk in wisdom by being filled with the _____.

Discuss

In the video Tony mentioned two types of holiness that we should keep in mind anytime we read a passage in the Bible about holiness.

What are they? Which of the two types does Ephesians 4–5 address?

Which of the two types should define your identity? Why?

When it comes to holiness, our culture often thinks of a caricatured holier-than-thou type of person. But Scripture paints a different picture.

What are some common cultural misconceptions of holiness?

Some people believe we find holiness when we isolate ourselves from others and from the world.

Why is isolationism not the same as holiness? How did Jesus demonstrate perfect holiness even while interacting with sinners?

Tony said, "The reason there's so little happiness in our world today is there's so little holiness in our world today." What did he mean? Do you believe that? Why or why not?

Our culture confuses love with four ideas: lust, tolerance, everything, and a feeling.

Why is each of these not true, Christ-honoring love?

How do we love?

Read Ephesians 5:2.

We love "as Christ loved us and gave himself up for us." Love involves compassion that leads to action.

Based on this Scripture, what's a biblical definition of *love?*

Be honest. When you think of the word love, what do you tend to think? Have you ever loved someone with a biblical kind of love?

Read aloud Ephesians 4:19-32 together as a small group. As you read, notice the sins Paul listed.

Pursuing holiness means identifying sinful behaviors and attitudes so that you can apply the put off/put on principle. You'll read more about this principle in the personal study titled "The Put Off/Put On Principle" this week. As God exposes sins in your life, you have the opportunity to put off those sins and in their place put on character traits that honors God.

What sins listed in this passage do you need to repent of?

Tony said in our pursuit of holiness, the three ways we're to walk are in love, in the light, and in wisdom.

What does it mean for you to live a holy life in each of the previous three ways—

at school?

on the job?

on your team?

Conclude the group session with the prayer activity on the following page.

Pray

This week could have exposed some areas in our lives that we need to work on. Thankfully, as we learned in week 3, we don't have to work alone. In fact, we would be foolish to think we could fight against our weaknesses by ourselves.

By this time your group should be comfortable enough with one another to confess areas of your lives in which you're weak. Divide into smaller groups by gender, men with men and women with women.

Read aloud James 5:16 together as a group.

> Confess your sins to one another and pray for one another, that you may be healed. The prayer of a righteous person has great power as it is working.
> **James 5:16**

Ask whether anyone is willing to share a weakness they're currently facing.

As you share requests and close in prayer, ask the Holy Spirit to give you success this week in the areas where sin is creeping in. Be sure to follow up with one another throughout the week.

Prayer Requests

Encourage members to complete "This Week's Plan" before the next group session.

This Week's Plan

Worship

[ ] Read your Bible. Complete the reading plan on page 92.

[ ] Spend time with God by engaging with the devotional experience on page 93.

[ ] Connect with God every day in prayer.

Personal Study

[ ] Read and interact with "Living in the Light" on page 94.

[ ] Read and interact with "The Put Off/Put On Principle" on page 98.

Application

[ ] Identify an area of your life that needs to change as a result of the truth you learned in this week's study.

[ ] Memorize Ephesians 5:2.

[ ] Connect over coffee with someone in the group. Talk with them about the areas of your life in which you need to pursue holiness more diligently.

[ ] Continue your journal. This week record your thoughts about your identity, especially in light of the truths you've explored in this study.

Did you miss the group session?
Video sessions available for purchase at *lifeway.com/ephesians*

91

Read

Read the following Scripture passages this week. Use the acronym HEAR and the space provided to record your thoughts or action steps.

Day 1: Ephesians 5:1-7

Day 2: Ephesians 5:8-14

Day 3: Ephesians 5:15-21

Day 4: Ephesians 5:22-33

Day 5: Ephesians 6:1-9

Day 6: Ephesians 6:10-17

Day 7: Ephesians 6:18-24

Reflect

DIFFERENT FROM THE WORLD

Do you bear a family resemblance to your Heavenly Father, or do you look like the world around you? Read Paul's words to the church in Ephesus:

> Be imitators of God, as beloved children.
> **Ephesians 5:1**

Imitating God is a practical way to describe holiness. It's easy for holiness to become an abstract and seemingly impossible ideal. In fact, however, it's a series of decisions, actions, attitudes, and thoughts that begin to look more and more like our Heavenly Father as we follow Christ the Son.

How do you look different from the world in the way you live? Is there a difference in the way you spend your money? Fill up your calendar? Use your free time? Talk to your spouse? Give your resources? Find contentment?

In your practical holiness you should be set apart from the world. This isn't a detachment, living life in isolation in a bunker to avoid all cultural influences. Holiness is intentionally living in such a way that others "may see your good deeds and glorify God on the day of visitation" (1 Pet. 2:12).

What if someone who was completely lost, apart from Christ, saw the way you lived? Would they be struck by your love, mercy, generosity, and contentment? Or would they say, "We're just the same"?

If you weren't able to speak, would others know by the way you live that you follow Jesus?

Personal Study 1

LIVING IN THE LIGHT

We learned in this week's group study that as followers of Jesus who are pursuing holiness, we're to walk in the light.

Let's dive a little deeper and learn what walking in the light means.

Read 1 John 1:7.

> If we walk in the light, as he is in the light, we have fellowship with
> one another, and the blood of Jesus his Son cleanses us from all sin.
> **1 John 1:7**

In the broader context of this verse (see vv. 5-10), John contrasted light with darkness. God is light. Sin is darkness. The ways of God are light. The ways of our flesh are darkness. Verse 7 doesn't tell us just to dip our toes in the light. It doesn't tell us just to practice in the light or look toward the light. We're commanded to walk in the light. Walking is an everyday activity, one that's always moving us forward. The cost of discipleship is that we don't simply turn our backs on our former lives and stay put. We're called to walk the other way in the light.

As we do this, "we have fellowship with one another." Fellowship is more than just a potluck at church or pizza with your small group. John took fellowship to another level by equating our relationship with others and our walking in the light. He did this because we can't have true fellowship with one another until we have true fellowship with Jesus. Our fellowship is rooted in our identity; we're all unworthy followers of the King who need daily grace.

How have you seen walking in the light affect fellowship?

How have you seen walking in the darkness affect fellowship?

Read Ephesians 5:8-9,13.

> At one time you were darkness, but now you are light in the Lord. Walk
> as children of light (for the fruit of light is found in all that is good and right
> and true). When anything is exposed by the light, it becomes visible.
> **Ephesians 5:8-9,13**

Tony pointed out in this week's video that in verse 8 Paul said, "At one time
you were darkness." Notice it's not "You were walking in darkness" (though
that's true). It's "You were darkness." Now, he said, "You are light in the
Lord." So your identity has changed. If your identity has changed, your
behaviors and attitudes should change too.

As followers of Christ, we know we're not supposed to live in darkness.
We're commanded not to pursue sin. But Paul took this a step further. He
called us not just to avoid darkness but to expose it as well. We have an
obligation both to avoid and to expose. It's as if we're standing in a dark
room with a flashlight, screaming to everyone else who'll hear, "Stay away

from that! See it? There it is! Get away! It's dangerous!" That's the warning we convey as we shine our light into the darkness.

In what areas of our culture does darkness seem to prevail?

What can you and your small group or local church do to expose the darkness?

Before we get too overwhelmed by the darkness and the way our culture around the world seems to be consumed by it, let's grab some hope.

Read John 1:1-5.

Verse 5 says this:

> The light shines in the darkness, and the darkness has not overcome it.
> **John 1:5**

When light shows up, darkness goes away. Don't believe me? Try standing in a dark room and turning on a light. Doesn't the darkness scatter? Doesn't it run? After 60 seconds does the darkness start encroaching back on its lost territory? No! The light continues to win.

Do you know whom "the light" is referring to in John 1:5? It's Jesus Himself. And He's already defeated death and darkness. Our King has won the battle, and we get to share in His spoils. We get to walk in the light!

Our Light, Jesus, said these words:

> You are the light of the world. A city set on a hill cannot be hidden. Nor do people light a lamp and put it under a basket, but on a stand, and it gives light to all in the house. In the same way, let your light shine before others, so that they may see your good works and give glory to your Father who is in heaven.
> **Matthew 5:14-16**

We, the church, are the light of the world. And our light can't be hidden unless we actively choose to hide it. And when our light comes into a place, "it gives light to all in the house" (v. 15).

Don't be overwhelmed by the darkness. Rather, fight against the darkness with the one thing that has the power to overcome it: light.

Personal Study 2

THE PUT OFF/PUT ON PRINCIPLE

In Ephesians 4–5 Paul urges us to put off lots of different activities.

Read again Ephesians 4:25-5:11.

In this passage Paul commands us to put off behaviors like lying, anger, stealing, corrupt talk, bitterness, slander, malice, filthiness, foolish talk, and crude joking.

We can work to stop doing these things. We can try to put them off. But the problem is that these behaviors are driven by our hearts. They're not simply actions existing in a bubble. They're driven by our motives and desires. So to stop the action without replacing it with an action that reorients our heart toward Jesus will cause a vacuum to form. When a vacuum forms in our heart, another behavior rushes in to take its place.

Have you ever heard of a dry drunk? This is someone who was formerly addicted to alcohol. They aren't addicted anymore, so they're technically considered dry. But although they haven't had a drop of alcohol, they've substituted another issue in its place. They don't drink, but they've got a short fuse. They don't drink, but they have explosive anger. They don't drink, but they're full of resentment.

Dry drunks have simply replaced one behavior with another, never addressing the root cause of their addiction: a heart that's bent on something other than God. So when one sinful behavior is removed and no God-honoring activity is put in its place, the heart remains unchanged.

So Paul said for each sin he listed, we must put on a new action:

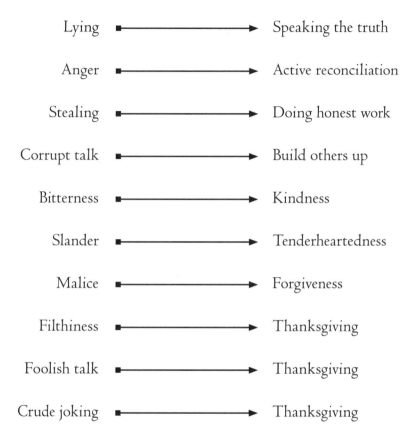

Lying ■——————————► Speaking the truth

Anger ■——————————► Active reconciliation

Stealing ■——————————► Doing honest work

Corrupt talk ■——————————► Build others up

Bitterness ■——————————► Kindness

Slander ■——————————► Tenderheartedness

Malice ■——————————► Forgiveness

Filthiness ■——————————► Thanksgiving

Foolish talk ■——————————► Thanksgiving

Crude joking ■——————————► Thanksgiving

**Have you ever known someone who changed their behavior,
but their heart remained the same? What action should that person
have substituted for the behavior they were trying to change?**

Ephesians 5:15 tells us:

Look carefully then how you walk, not as unwise but as wise.
Ephesians 5:15

There are some behaviors we simply need to replace with God-honoring ones. There are other behaviors, addictions in particular, we need to be even more aggressive with. Instead of simply replacing the sinful habit with a God-honoring one, we may need to completely remove ourselves from the environment. That's part of walking in wisdom, as Paul admonished in Ephesians 5:15. Be diligent with every step and pursue wisdom. If Paul were writing to you today, maybe he would say something like "You need to put off that job." Or "You need to put off that relationship." Or maybe "You need to put off that whole city. Get out of there. Its pull on your heart is too strong."

Is there an area of your life that you need to start looking at more carefully?

Who can help you live more wisely? Record their name(s) below.

Why is it important to have someone help you walk in wisdom?

Read Romans 13:11-12.

Besides this you know the time, that the hour has come for you to wake from sleep. For salvation is nearer to us now than when we first believed. The night is far gone; the day is at hand. So then let us cast off the works of darkness and put on the armor of light.
Romans 13:11-12

Friend, it's time to wake up. If we have behaviors in our lives that need to change, let's get creative and find ways to combat our sin. "The hour has come" for us to "wake from sleep" (v. 11). No more slumbering! If there are behaviors that need to be put off, let's do the hard work of cleansing our lives of the activities that are dragging us down. Let's find the opposite behavior that, through the power of the Holy Spirit, will work to change our hearts.

Romans 13:11-12 remind us that none of us know the hour when Jesus will come. But we can say with great confidence that we're closer to His second coming today than we were yesterday. So let's buckle down and pursue holiness in character and behavior. As we follow Christ, we'll look more and more like Him. As the affections of our hearts and the source of our identities are rooted in Christ, the more evidence we'll see of spiritual fruit.

If you asked a good friend, "What areas of my spiritual life do I need to work on?" what would he or she say?

What opposite behaviors can you put on in the areas your friend suggested? How can you do that

As we continue through this study, may we regularly pray with the psalmist:

> Create in me a clean heart, O God,
>   and renew a right spirit within me.
> **Psalm 51:10**

Be Strong in Christ

Whether or not you know it, you're in a battle every day. And this is the most dangerous battle you could imagine. It's one that can take your identity and twist it in all kinds of directions. You may be tempted to think the battle is against flesh and blood. But this battle isn't against any forces we can see.

Weapons of the flesh aren't going to work against this enemy. You've got to be equipped with armor of a different kind if you're going to be ready for the enemy who's coming your way.

Like a warrior in an army, you don't have to head to the battlefield unprotected. Thankfully, you aren't left to fight on your own or forge your own battle gear. God has provided armor for you. You're going to need to utilize every piece of the armor God gives you to protect every part of yourself, even though (spoiler alert!) the ultimate battle has already been won.

This final week of study will help equip you to fight daily for your identity as unseen forces all around you strive to rob and destroy you.

Start

We've made it to the final week of our study of Ephesians. Last week we studied the biblical concept of holiness. We saw that the Bible teaches a holiness that looks different from what the world thinks holiness is. We also saw that true, Christ-honoring love is action-oriented. It's not simply a lust or a feeling.

> **As you read "Walking in the Light" in your personal study, did you identify any areas of the culture that you would like to expose with the light (see Eph. 5:13)?**
>
> **How could your group get involved in doing that?**

In our final week of study, Tony is going to focus on the final chapter of Ephesians. We'll look together at the armor God provides for us to fight against unseen forces that are waging war against us. There's an all-out war against our identity and holiness. It's time to suit up for battle.

Pray that God will open your hearts and minds as you watch video session 6.

Watch

Use the space below to follow along and take notes as you watch video session 6.

We're made for _____.

There's an _____ element to this battle.

There's a _____ element.

There's an _____ element.

There's a _____ element.

Our _____ is in our union with Christ. It's in our identity
in Christ.

Don't go into the battle without a _____. Don't go into
the battle without a sword.

The first step to fighting spiritual warfare is to really _____
a battle's going on.

Discuss

Use the following statements and questions to discuss the video.

In this week's video Tony introduced the armor of God we need to fight against spiritual powers that seek to thwart and destroy us.

Were you ever in a physical fight as a kid? How did things turn out?

We may be prone to think Satan is at work only in events like terrorist attacks. But in reality Satan would love nothing more than to destroy the everyday relationships you have in your local church and in your family.

Read Ephesians 6:10.

Based on what you've learned so far in this study, brainstorm together with the group some ways you can "be strong in the Lord."

What habits did you start during this study that you can continue afterward?

Read Ephesians 6:11-13.

We can't fight spiritual battles using our own strength, our own resources, or our own abilities. The strength mentioned in verses 10-13 implies that the devil can truly be defeated. That's great news!

On a scale of 1 to 10, how equipped do you feel to do daily battle against Satan?

1	2	3	4	5	6	7	8	9	10
Not at all									Fully ready

What would help increase your number?

Read Ephesians 6:14-17.

Paul mentioned these pieces of armor in this passage: the belt of truth (see v. 14), the breastplate of righteousness (see v. 14), the gospel shoes (see v. 15), the shield of faith, (see v. 16) the helmet of salvation (see v. 17), and the sword of the Spirit (see v. 17).

Which pieces of armor are defensive? Explain the value and meaning of each piece.

What's the offensive weapon? Why is this important?

What area of your life is most vulnerable to attack?

Which piece of armor would strengthen your offense or defense?

Tony said in the video, "If you're not in the battle by daily Bible reading, meditation, and using your Bible reading as a catalyst for your prayers, then start."

What does your Bible-reading plan look like? How are you disciplining yourself to read the Bible regularly?

Has the weekly reading plan been helpful for you? In what ways?

What difference have you noticed in your life when you spend consistent time in Scripture?

Conclude the group session with the prayer activity on the following page.

Pray

Spiritual battles are going on all around us all the time. Satan and his army would love to wreck our witness, our jobs, our churches, our families, and our communities.

Share ways you feel that any one of these areas is under spiritual attack in your life right now.

As you close the group session, pray specifically for anyone who shared a difficulty. Pray for one another by name and for each situation in detail. When we pray specifically, God answers specifically, and we know precisely how to thank Him when He comes through for us.

Ask the Holy Spirit to guide each of you to live battle-ready.

Prayer Requests

Encourage members to complete "This Week's Plan" on their own. Begin the conversation now, if your group hasn't already, about what you'll study next. You can find suggested resources at *lifeway.com*.

This Week's Plan

Worship

[ ] Continue to read your Bible daily. Complete the reading plan on page 110. Consider reading Paul's next letter, Philippians.

[ ] Spend time with God by engaging with the devotional experience on page 111.

[ ] Connect with God every day in prayer.

Personal Study

[ ] Read and interact with "Growing Up on the Battlefield" on page 112.

[ ] Read and interact with "Should I Stay, or Should I Go?" on page 116.

Application

[ ] Identify an area of your life that needs to change as a result of the truth you learned in this week's study.

[ ] Memorize Ephesians 6:10-11.

[ ] Connect over coffee with someone in the group. Talk with them about the areas of your life where you need to put on the armor of God.

[ ] Continue your journal. This week record ways you see Satan working against you, trying to undermine your identity in Christ.

Did you miss the group session?
Video sessions available for purchase at *lifeway.com/ephesians*

109

Read

Read the following Scripture passages this week. Use the acronym HEAR and the space provided to record your thoughts or action steps.

Day 1: Ephesians 6:10-20

Day 2: Ephesians 1

Day 3: Ephesians 2

Day 4: Ephesians 3

Day 5: Ephesians 4

Day 6: Ephesians 5

Day 7: Ephesians 6

Reflect

I'LL TELL MY DAD!

When I was in elementary school, the phrase "I'll tell my dad!" was the ultimate trump card. It would end every argument, fuss, and squabble.

When it comes to the battles we face every day, we can't fight them with our own strength, our own weapons, or our own reputation. We can truly do nothing apart from Christ. Read Jesus' words:

> I am the vine; you are the branches. Whoever abides in me and I in him,
> he it is that bears much fruit, for apart from me you can do nothing.
> **John 15:5**

What challenges do you need to address by abiding in Jesus?

The next time Satan tempts you, speak these words to him: "I'll tell my dad!" God will have your back every single time. He will never leave you alone. He will never leave you exposed in battle with your enemy. And the moment you call on Him is the moment you'll realize He's right beside you:

> Fear not, for I am with you;
>   be not dismayed, for I am your God;
> I will strengthen you, I will help you,
>   I will uphold you with my righteous right hand.
> **Isaiah 41:10**

What area of your life right now is marked by fear?

How can you apply the truth of God's presence to your fear?

Personal Study 1

GROWING UP ON THE BATTLEFIELD

From the earliest moments of our lives, we're in the middle of spiritual warfare. In fact, we've already seen that God's Word clearly teaches that we're not only targets of spiritual attack but also natural enemies of God.

We can see the battle in everyday life. Sin comes naturally. It's easy. Children don't have to be taught disobedience. Disobedience comes naturally, but we have to be taught to do what's right. We have to be taught the gospel.

Whether or not you have children of your own now, you were once a child, and you're around other children in your church and maybe those of extended family or friends. Other people, especially parents, have a profound influence on our spiritual development.

Was it easy or difficult to trust, obey, and respect your parents? Why or why not?

For better or for worse, in what ways did your family affect your spiritual growth and your perspective on God?

Read Ephesians 6:1-4.

How is obedience related to the gospel? How is honor related to the gospel?

The apostle Paul reminded the Christians in Ephesus that the front lines of spiritual warfare are in the home. We must be intentional in order to have Christ-centered homes. As parents, we must share the gospel and exercise Christlike authority. As children, we have to learn obedience.

This family relationship, though marred by sin, is our first picture of a relationship with God. We're children of a perfect, loving Heavenly Father who's worthy of all honor and complete obedience. He's wise and knows what's best for our well-being, joy, and safety.

As Christians, we must learn to trust and obey our Heavenly Father, even when we don't understand or like it. We may not see the benefit or reason in the moment; in fact, we may never understand, but God is good and can be trusted. The gospel message is that He gave His only Son out of His love for us so that we can live eternally as part of His family (see John 3:16).

Paul spoke not only to children but also to parents. He encouraged fathers not to provoke their children. (The same Greek word for *fathers* in this verse is translated *parents* in Hebrews 11:23, so if you're a mom, don't think you get a free pass on this command.) The way we lead our children has far-reaching spiritual effects on their lives, and if they walk around feeling provoked and discouraged, we're creating a barrier between them and God.

Was there ever a time when your parents provoked you? Describe the discouraging effects that treatment had on you as a child and as you grew into adulthood.

We should work to be "fair, loving, and consistent"[1] in both our love and our discipline. What are some ways parents could stir up anger and resentment in children?

How can an angry home be fertile ground for spiritual warfare?

What's an example of loving discipline?

Read Deuteronomy 6:5-9.

Long before Paul wrote to the Ephesians, Moses wrote to the Israelites. Notice that God's message to families hasn't changed. We're to teach kids to love God with all their heart, soul, and might. The passage says to talk about the things of God "when you sit in your house, and when you walk by the way, and when you lie down, and when you rise" (v. 7).

Record practical ways you can teach and model God's love in the rhythm of your daily life.

When you sit in your house:

When you walk by the way:

When you lie down:

When you rise:

When we think about the word *teaching*, we tend to think of lectures. So to teach our kids as they rise may make us think we have to be prepared to deliver a sermon as soon their feet hit the floor each morning. But our actions are just as important as our words.

In what ways are you modeling a life of obedience? A life of honor?

If you're failing to show honor or to be obedient to authority, what do you need to do to model repentance?

If you have children, how have they seen you place value on your relationship with God and your relationship with them, not just on their obedience to you?

What will you do to intentionally teach children the gospel, whether in your own home, in your community, or in your church?

Spend time in prayer, thanking God for your family and asking Him to heal any relational wounds for the sake of the gospel. Pray for discernment in how best to train up a generation of Christ followers who'll walk in faith no matter what they face in their day-to-day lives.

1. Tony Merida, *Christ-Centered Exposition: Exalting Jesus in Ephesians* (Nashville: Holman Reference, 2014), 152.

Personal Study 2

SHOULD I STAY, OR SHOULD I GO?

When temptations comes our way, should we stand and fight or turn and run? Do we stand strong like a soldier or run away? Do we fight, or does God fight for us? Do we suit up with armor or rest in our identity in Christ?

The answer is "It depends." We'll look at three different scenarios, along with three very different responses that Scripture calls us to.

God Will Fight for Us

Read at least one of the following passages: Exodus 14:14; Deuteronomy 3:22; 2 Chronicles 20:17.

Even when our life seems hopeless and we feel overwhelmed, in the moments and seasons when we're tempted to doubt God's presence and doubt that He even cares, we can trust that God fights our battles for us. He will supply all our needs "according to His riches in glory in Christ Jesus" (Phil. 4:19). He makes good plans for us even when those plans won't come to fruition for years (see Jer. 29:11). His ways are higher than our ways (see Isa. 55:8-9).

We can ask God to fight for us when we're discouraged or afraid.

When have you needed the reminder that God fights your battles?

What situations in life bring you great discouragement?

Describe a time in your life when you were afraid of what was coming.

How can you use the truth of the previous passages to conquer your fear and to rely on God?

Stand and Fight

Even though God fights for us, we're also called to stand and fight Satan.

Read at least one of the following passages, noticing the verbs that call us to action: Ephesians 6:11-18; James 1:12; 1 Peter 5:8-9.

Standing and fighting are different from asking God to fight for us. We're called to stand and fight when we're under trial. When we're suffering, we should fight. Satan is prowling around like a lion ready to devour us, but if we stand firm (knowing it's by God's strength we stand, not our own), we'll win. Daily, sometimes hourly, we're called to fight. It's through suffering that God forms us into the image of Jesus (see Rom. 8:28-29) and creates a ministry for us through which we can serve others (see 2 Cor. 1:3-7).

When have you stood your ground and fought Satan?

Has there been a cause for which you've stood up and fought? Did you feel as if Satan were working against you?

How does the truth that others are suffering around the world (see I Pet. 5:9) embolden your faith and your fight?

We're called to stand, resist, and fight the devil.

Turn and Flee

We're also called to turn and flee from temptations when they come our way, especially sexual sins.

Read 1 Corinthians 6:18; 10:13.

The message of these verses is pretty clear. Flee! Run away! When you're sexually tempted, run. When you're tempted, drawn back toward things you've struggled with in the past, whether that's addictions (substances or otherwise) or relationships, run. When your flesh calls out to you, it's no time to stand and fight. Remove yourself from the situation. Don't put yourself where you're likely to stumble.

First Corinthians 10:13 indicates that if God is providing a means of escape, we should take Him up on it. He doesn't provide us an escape route so that we can stare at it. Run through the open door.

When have you needed to run from a tempting situation or person? Were you given a way out?

What time in your life did you decide not to run?

What would a better practical response have been?

Now you know the different situations that warrant different responses:

1. God will fight our battles when we're discouraged and afraid.
2. We should stand and fight when we're facing Satan and are under trials.
3. We should flee when we're faced with temptation.

What situations are you facing right now?

What response is needed?

Leader Guide

Opening and Closing Group Sessions

Always try to engage each person at the beginning of a group session. Once a person speaks, even if only to answer a generic question, he or she is more likely to speak up later about more personal matters.

You may want to begin each session by reviewing the previous week's personal study. This review provides context for the new session and opportunities to share relevant experiences, application, or truths learned between sessions. Then set up the theme of the study to prepare personal expectations.

Always open and close the session with prayer, recognizing that only the Holy Spirit provides understanding and transformation in our lives. (The prayer suggestions provided in each session help focus members on Scripture, key truths, and personal application from the week's teaching.)

Remember that your goal isn't just meaningful discussion but discipleship.

Session 1: The Struggle in Ephesus

The questions in the "Start" section engage people in a fun conversation to get them talking and begin thinking about personal identity.

> **How have you seen someone's behavior change when they started a new relationship?**

> **How does your relationship with Jesus change the way you live your life?**

This opening series of questions is the leader's chance to be honest and lead the way in authenticity. Your relationship with God isn't perfect. Talk about ways you're continuing to learn obedience. This way you create the opportunity for others to share honestly.

Some people in the group may not be believers yet. Be sure to make them feel welcome. Let them know your group is a safe place for them to be open and honest. Remind them that everybody has a faith story, whether or not they're a follower of Jesus. Give them freedom to share, ask questions, and share frustrations as the study progresses.

Read Ephesians 1:1-2 aloud with the group.

Always keep God's Word central during the group session. This prevents people from getting off track and veering into speculation or opinion. Even though Tony teaches on the video, the goal is for people to walk away knowing what the Bible says, not just what a pastor or a group leader says. Asking group members to read aloud also invites greater participation and encourages confidence as they "lead" in that moment.

How does knowing you're covered in grace and peace affect the way you see yourself? Receive criticism? View success? Vacation?

This begin a series of questions to help group members examine their lives in light of Scripture and make personal application.

What are your hopes or expectations for this study of Ephesians?

This question is simple but important in three ways: (1) It provides clues on where people are in their spiritual journeys. (2) It helps people evaluate their spiritual lives and be intentional about their growth. (3) It provides encouragement and accountability when members know that nobody is perfect and everyone has room to grow.

Session 1 closes with a time for members to pray for one another, especially about the hopes they've shared for the next six weeks.

Session 2: New Life in Christ

Start by reviewing the previous group session and what people have read, studied, or journaled during the week. This session is unique in that it may be the first time some people in the group have read an entire book of the Bible. Point out the importance of Scripture as the Word of God and the fact that it's best understood in context. Understanding the context of what we discuss helps prevent us from creating our own opinions about God and the Bible instead of letting the Bible shape our understanding of God.

Make the transition from the video teaching to discussion with a short summary statement. Don't reteach the lesson. Keep your transition minimal, using the provided sentence as your guide. This is true for any of the statements provided between questions. Feel free to say as much or as little as needed in the group, but remember that your intent is to facilitate discussion, not reteach.

Why is it significant that Paul referred to us as dead people?

Point out the sobering reality that before our relationship with Jesus, we were dead. We were without any hope of life. We pursued our own means by our own path. Some people in the group may claim that they didn't feel as if they were doing bad things all the time. The language in the text may seem harsh, but it emphasizes the severity of our need for salvation. No matter how we feel, God is opening our eyes to the truth about our identities with and without Christ.

If our works don't save us, then what purpose do they serve?

Be sure people understand that we're not working to be accepted by Christ but because we've received His great grace. God has already accepted us in Christ. Because God has brought us from death to life, we want to serve Him. Our works are expressions of gratitude, not attempts to gain favor. When we were dead, we couldn't do anything to gain life. Our actions reveal that we've been given new life.

Why is it vital to know that salvation is a gift, not a prize?

A prize is earned. A gift is received. The fact that we can't earn salvation is a key truth from Ephesians 2:8-10. Instead of pouring out judgment on us, God poured it out on Jesus so that we could have eternal life with Him. This is the good news. We were destined for wrath but instead received a gift.

What makes Christianity distinct among all world religions and philosophies?

How would you explain the good news of the gospel?

Be sure group members can clearly articulate the gospel and our need for salvation by grace through faith in Jesus. He's the only way to move from spiritual death to spiritual life. Salvation and eternal life can't be earned.

This is a great opportunity for a gospel presentation. Don't assume everyone in the group is saved. Take advantage of this time to share your testimony and to help group members think about their own transformations from death to life.

The three questions provided at the end of "Discuss" are also intended to help introduce the fact that although your identity as a Christian is a matter of personal faith, God works through other Christians to share the gospel and to help us grow in spiritual maturity. Session 3 will emphasize the relational nature of our identities as part of the church.

Session 3: New Life in Community

Paul described us as "separated from Christ, alienated" (Eph. 2:12). What does it mean to be alienated from others?

From whom do you feel alienated at this time in your life?

What would reconciliation look like for you?

Be sure this doesn't become a gripe or gossip session. The intent is to focus attention on our own lives. It's easy to affirm the value of reconciliation or grace in theory or when we're the recipients. It's much more difficult to wrestle with the same truth when it applies to the painful areas of our lives.

To be alienated from someone means a relationship should exist but doesn't. We can be alienated from our spouse, kids, parents, or friends. But in this context we aren't alienated from someone we've never met. In a similar vein, we were created to have a relationship with God, but we're operating as aliens until we're reconciled with Him.

Help member understand that a Gentile is a non-Jew. Anyone in the group who wasn't not born of Jewish heritage would be considered a Gentile. This is significant, because while the apostle Peter was sent to the Jews, the apostle Paul was sent to evangelize and disciple Gentiles (see Acts 22:21).

What's significant about "the blood of Christ" (Eph. 2:13)?

Based on these verses, what should we do when there's a wall between us and someone else?

The spilling of Jesus' blood on the cross was the pouring out of His life. Only through His death, which paid the ransom for our sin, are we able to be reconciled with God and others.

Although we should work toward reconciliation with others, in certain instances we need to protect ourselves and create boundaries. This happens on a case-by-case basis, but be aware that boundaries are healthy and don't mean reconciliation hasn't happened. Past sins can have lifelong consequences, some of which are good for both the offended and the offender. Having a heart ready to forgive is an important step, reflecting a heart that's been reconciled to God. Be sensitive when past hurt has happened.

> **Which of the three pictures of community described in Ephesians 2:19-22 do you need the most in your life right now?**

> **How would you respond to someone who says, "I love Jesus, but I don't love His church"?**

Encourage honesty, especially if people in the group have been hurt by the church. But help the group see that to say you love Jesus but don't love His church is offensive to Jesus. It's like telling a husband, "I love you, but I can't stand your wife." That's offensive to the husband because he and his wife are one. Not loving the church is similarly unhealthy because Jesus died for the church, His body.

However, also keep in mind that people who say they don't love the church have often been hurt by a local church or by its pastor. It's unfortunate, but be cautious about pushing too hard on people who are wary of joining a local body of believers.

> **What relationship is strained or broken in your life, especially a relationship with another Christian?**

Review specific action steps in members' efforts to seek reconciliation. Remind everyone of the importance of maintaining healthy boundaries while freely extending the grace they've received in Christ.

Session 4: Pursuing Unity in Christ

Before the group arrives, think back through the previous three weeks—both what you've learned and what you've experienced as a result. Be ready to start the session by openly sharing about your own walk with Jesus thus far in the study. Help group members consider progress toward the benefits they said they hoped to get from this study This is also a way to ensure that people are keeping the whole study of Ephesians in context while also applying what they've learned. It's a great opportunity for you, as the leader, to gauge members' growth in spiritual maturity.

> **What evidence have you seen that your church is characterized by a supernatural unity?**
>
> **What action steps have you personally taken to fight against disunity?**

As in previous sessions, the aim of questions like these isn't to gripe or gossip but to celebrate positives and to consider practical ways individuals can assist in solutions to any perceived problems. Remind people that it's every church member's responsibility to seek unity, not just the paid staff.

> **How would you define the characteristics Paul used to describe the Christian life—humility, gentleness, patience, and love?**
>
> **What's the opposite of each of those qualities?**
>
> **How have you seen each of these contributing to or detracting from eagerly maintaining "the unity of the Spirit in the bond of peace" (Eph. 4:3)?**

Be prepared to elaborate on definitions by providing real-life examples of characteristics of Christian maturity and of the opposite of each trait: humility versus self-centeredness, gentleness versus harshness or hotheadedness, patience versus thinking our agenda is always right, love versus treating people as a burden and pain.

It can't be overemphasized that people don't drift toward unity but away from it. This is true of all aspects of Christian maturity.

When was the last time you maintained unity by having a difficult conversation with someone?

As always, go first. You set the tone for what's safe by what you share. If you share only surface-level platitudes, others won't feel that the group is safe for them to be open and honest. But if you share authentically, you'll encourage others to do the same.

If you don't know of a time when you initiated a conversation like this, admit that this is an area in which you need to grow as a Christian. Share a time when someone initiated a conversation with you and the result.

These conversations may be related to the three main elements Tony mentioned that unite a church, or they may also be related to essential doctrines of the Christian faith. It's recommended that you obtain a copy of your church's core beliefs to accurately discuss any matters of doctrine that sometimes cause divisions among Christians but that unite your church.

How would you use a story from your life to help someone who says they don't need church see the mutual benefit of community?

Begin moving toward a time of prayer by helping people reflect again on their personal experiences and testimonies as part of a community of faith.

Session 5: Pursuing Holiness in Christ

Start the group session by reviewing the previous week and by reminding everyone that the purpose of the church isn't to create uniformity that makes us the same but, rather, unity that gives us the same purpose and passion: growing together in grace and going to others with the gospel.

What are the two types of holiness? Which of the two types does Ephesians 4–5 address?

Which of the two types should define your identity? Why?

Our positional holiness is who God has declared us to be, and this never changes. It's rooted in the finished work of Jesus, not the ever-changing, ever-challenging process of growing in our relationship with Jesus in a fallen world.

Be sure to read the room at this point. If some members still seem confused, spend more time asking questions about holiness and our identity. It's important that members understand that their identity isn't in what they do but in who God has declared them to be in Christ.

What are some common cultural misconceptions of holiness?

Why is isolationism not the same as holiness? How did Jesus demonstrate perfect holiness even while interacting with sinners?

This is important for everyone to understand because we won't fulfill the Great Commission and we can't be good missionaries if we avoid contact with people. When we talk about holiness, aren't talking about isolationism. In fact, many teachings in Scripture command us to do things for one another. These commands can't be obeyed in isolation.

Tony said, "The reason there's so little happiness in our world today is there's so little holiness in our world today." What did he mean? Do you believe that? Why or why not?

This is an opportunity for group members to process what they've heard and to engage with an idea that may be surprising or new to them. Often people think happiness and holiness are at opposite ends of a spectrum. It's common for some Christians to believe God isn't concerned with our happiness, meaning happiness is nonspiritual and of the flesh. If people have never considered happiness and holiness as being related, help them recognize the joy and freedom in trusting that our Creator knows what's best for our lives. Sin always leads to brokenness.

Our culture confuses love with four ideas: lust, tolerance, everything, and a feeling.

Why is each of these not true, Christ-honoring love?

Based on Ephesians 5:2, what's a biblical definition of *love?*

Answers should be something like this: Christ-centered love is sacrificially giving up yourself for the good of others as an act of worship to God. Lead the group in a candid discussion about:

1. Lust versus seeking to serve, not be served
2. Tolerance versus speaking the truth in love
3. A feeling versus a commitment

Each week you have a moment to go first in your confession and application of the Scripture passage being studied. You set the bar for vulnerability and honesty. The way you conclude the session will result in superficiality or in-depth application.

Session 6: Be Strong in Christ

This is your final session of the study, so come prepared for three things.

1. Be prepared to review session 5 and discuss session 6, as usual.
2. Be prepared to review the entire six-week study of the Book of Ephesians.
3. Be prepared to discuss plans for what the group will study next.

Were you ever in a physical fight as a kid? How did things turn out?

This question is a simple way to get to know more about one another. Most answers are likely to be funny childhood skirmishes, but be prepared for the possibility that someone will share a more painful, serious experience. In either case be sure your mood is appropriate for transitioning to the fact that all conflict is a result of sin and has a spiritual dynamic.

Based on what you've learned so far in this study, brainstorm together with the group some ways you can "be strong in the Lord" (Eph. 6:10).

What habits did you start during this study that you can continue afterward?

Accountability, Scripture reading, and prayer are vital disciplines in the Christian life. These elements have been regular parts not only of the group sessions but also of each group member's personal study between group sessions. Be sure to point out that another valuable spiritual habit is community. A small group that meets consistently is a spiritual habit that group members can continue. Though we tend to think of habits as a personal disciplines, corporate disciplines are important as well.

On a scale of I to I0 (I being not at all, I0 being fully ready), how equipped do you feel to do daily battle against Satan?

Questions on a scale of 1 to 10 or multiple-choice questions are an easy way everyone can engage in the conversation while also beginning to think more deeply about the question—in this case, readiness for spiritual warfare.

We need to realize our dependency on Christ. Our strength is in the Lord and in our union with Christ. Our strength is supercharged by our communion with Christ as we connect with Him though prayer and Scripture.

Remind members that we aren't designed to fight completely alone. Fighting in the context of community means we can consistently win. Encourage people to form pairs or work in groups of three or four as you discuss more personal application and pray for one another.

> **Which pieces of armor are defensive? What's the offensive weapon? What area of your life is most vulnerable to attack?**

Discuss each piece of armor and areas of weakness in our lives. Help one another create a battle plan for ongoing spiritual disciplines and accountability in areas of weakness.

Emphasize the essential nature of God's Word for the Christian life. Discuss ways reading the Book of Ephesians over the past six weeks has had an impact on daily life. Share and ask for any tips that help people prioritize and enjoy Scripture reading.

Ask members to identify the main things they've learned and applied from this study of Ephesians. Be sure to inform group members of plans for the next Bible study.

Close by praying for one another in pairs or small groups.

Tips for Leading a Small Group

Prayerfully Prepare

Prepare for each group session with prayer. Ask the Holy Spirit to work through you and the group discussion as you point to Jesus each week through God's Word.

REVIEW the weekly material and group questions ahead of time.

PRAY for each person in the group.

Minimize Distractions

Do everything in your ability to help people focus on what's most important: connecting with God, with the Bible, and with one another. Create a comfortable environment. If group members are uncomfortable, they'll be distracted and therefore not engaged in the group experience. Take into consideration seating, temperature, lighting, refreshments, surrounding noise, and general cleanliness.

At best, thoughtfulness and hospitality show guests and group members they're welcome and valued in whatever environment you choose to gather. At worst, people may never notice your effort, but they're also not distracted.

Include Others

Your goal is to foster a community in which people are welcome just as they are but encouraged to grow spiritually. Always be aware of opportunities to include and invite.

INVITE new people to join your group.

INCLUDE anyone who visits the group.

Encourage Discussion

A good small-group experience has the following characteristics.

EVERYONE PARTICIPATES. Encourage everyone to ask questions, share responses, or read aloud.

NO ONE DOMINATES—NOT EVEN THE LEADER. Be sure your time speaking as a leader takes up less than half your time together as a group. Politely guide discussion if anyone dominates.

NOBODY IS RUSHED THROUGH QUESTIONS. Don't feel that a moment of silence is a bad thing. People often need time to think about their responses to questions they've just heard or to gain courage to share what God is stirring in their hearts.

INPUT IS AFFIRMED AND FOLLOWED UP. Make sure you point out something true or helpful in a response. Don't just move on. Build community with follow-up questions, asking how other people have experienced similar things or how a truth has shaped their understanding of God and the Scripture you're studying. People are less likely to speak up if they fear that you don't actually want to hear their answers or that you're looking for only a certain answer.

GOD AND HIS WORD ARE CENTRAL. Opinions and experiences can be helpful, but God has given us the truth. Trust Scripture to be the authority and God's Spirit to work in people's lives. You can't change anyone, but God can. Continually point people to the Word and to active steps of faith.

KEEP CONNECTING

Think of ways to connect with group members during the week. Participation during the group session is always improved when members spend time connecting with one another outside the group sessions. The more people are comfortable with and involved in one another's lives, the more they'll look forward to being together. When people move beyond being friendly to truly being friends who form a community, they come to each session eager to engage instead of merely attending.

Encourage group members with thoughts, commitments, or questions from the session by connecting through emails, texts, and social media.

Build deeper friendships by planning or spontaneously inviting group members to join you outside your regularly scheduled group time for meals; fun activities; and projects around your home, church, or community.

Group Information

NAME   **CONTACT**

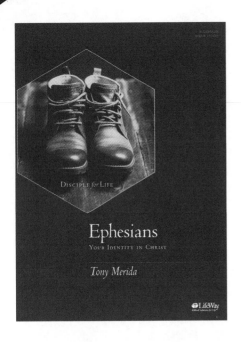

NOW THAT YOU UNDERSTAND YOUR IDENTITY IN CHRIST,
BE INTENTIONAL ABOUT GROWING AS A DISCIPLE.

Disciples Path is a series of six resources founded on Jesus' model of discipleship. It provides an intentional path for transformational discipleship created by experienced disciple-makers across the nation. While most small-group studies facilitate transformation through relationship and information, these disciple-making resources do it through the principles of modeling, practicing, and multiplying:

- Leaders model a biblical life.
- Disciples follow and practice from the leader's example.
- Disciples become disciple makers and multiply through Disciples Path.

Learn more at *disciplespath.com*

LifeWay